CARRIE ON

A MEMOIR

CARRIE WHITWORTH

Edited by
DEB NOACK

PREFACE

"You should write a book." I wish I could count the number of times my mother said this to me. She also would ask, "How do you keep falling into shit and come out smelling like roses?" She's gone now, but I hear her words louder than I ever did when she was alive.

She is the main inspiration for this book. My age, along with my recent battle with a life-threatening illness, also inspired me to record my story while I still could. I write it for future generations who will never get to meet me in person. It's a physical document that proves I was here. I've always struggled with feeling that I don't matter. Writing this book makes me realize, I do matter—even if it wasn't always to the people I most wanted to acknowledge me. If these stories inspire or help someone who has faced some of the same life challenges, that will be a bonus.

My youngest son told me he would probably not read this book. He said he wasn't into memoirs. He thinks they are a bit narcissistic. It was hard to argue with his opinion. It's a good thing I didn't write it for him.

I grew up in Maine. The core of who I am was created there. All I ever wanted to be was a mom. I believe it's because I had such beautiful role models. My mother and her mother taught me how to raise children. They showed me how to love. My grandmother was the closest thing to an angel I have ever met. I never heard her say a bad thing about anyone. When she died, three of her grandchildren spoke at her funeral. I was one of them.

None of us knew what the other was going to say. All three of us mentioned that we believed we were her favorite. Imagine having 14 grandchildren and every one of them felt they were the favorite? What an amazing grandmother; I've always been in awe of her. Just the mention of her name brings back so many fond memories. Walking into her home was such a pleasant experience. She always had something special in the oven for us. My favorite was her pork pie. It had ground pork mixed with potatoes and special spices inside the flakiest pie crust I have ever eaten. She also made many of our dresses when we were toddlers. My oldest sister Jayme always had blue dresses, mine were yellow and my younger sister Tammy had pink. She made dresses for my cousins as well. My grandmother was so talented, and her gifts were treasured. She made us collectable dolls when we became adults. Each doll had a ceramic head and was wearing a christening gown. The details were breathtaking. I still have mine today. My grandmother's crocheting and knitting skills were just as impressive. My keepsakes include blankets and quilts from her, and I treasure them all as well as my fond memories of her.

My sister Jayme, myself and my cousin on Easter Sunday all wearing handmade dresses and coats by my grandmother.

Once I began having my own children, she gave me some advice that I have shared many times with new mothers. She told me that no matter what I did as a mother, so long as I loved my kids, they would turn out all right. As I look at my kids today, I realize she was right.

My children are my resume. Each time I gave birth, I grew another heart. My kids are the best things I have ever created. I was far from the mother I would have liked to be but, despite my flaws, all my children turned out to be amazing humans. They are now raising little humans of their own and doing an incredible job!

When my children were growing up, I told them that it did not matter to me "what" they decided to become, it only mattered "who" they became. All of them have become better people than I could ever claim to be. My pride runs deep.

Everyone has a story. I hope you write yours. Write it while you still can. You don't need to publish it if you don't want to; just write it. You don't need to be a writer. Just put it on paper. Write down your memories so they can be shared with future generations. They will appreciate it.

Fair warning: this book contains some adult content. As difficult as it may be to read, I hope it will also help some readers start a difficult conversation regarding abuse. It is also my hope that, while reading this book, you find some humor, inspiration and value.

CHAPTER 1

*W*e finally boarded our plane. You could hear the clicking from the seatbelts as people found their seats and settled in for our long "red eye" flight to my hometown, South Portland, Maine. As we waited for our aircraft to taxi, I was feeling so many emotions. The purpose of this trip was to attend my father's memorial service. It had been over three months since his passing, but due to Covid, his services had been delayed. My father spent the last year of his life alone in a nursing home for veterans. He received excellent care but was away from everyone he loved. Covid robbed us of precious time with our dad. Because of Covid, my father took his last breath without any of his five children by his side. This made me both angry and sad. I needed to get past these emotions in order to grieve.

It was possible that this trip could be the last time we fly back to my hometown. Up until now, my parents had been the primary reason we returned to visit. They are both gone now. When we leave this time, I won't just be saying goodbye to my hometown; I will also be saying goodbye to so many childhood memories. For now, I focused on spending time with my daughters and their families. I was excited to see my nieces and nephews who we rarely had an opportunity to see. As is often the case, these gatherings contain a silver lining. Along with the anger and sadness, my heart was full of anticipation.

On the day of my father's service, everyone arrived safely and made it to the church on time. I managed to control my emotions and was able to read the following eulogy I had written:

For those of you who don't know me, my name is Carrie Whitworth. I am the second of five children of Jim and Peggy.

My siblings and I would like to thank you all for being here today. Whether you knew my dad or are here to just support us, we appreciate you.

I could stand up here today and tell you what a great dad my father was. I'm not going to, but he was. I could tell you what a great papa he was... because he was. Those two roles are probably the titles he was most proud of. Everyone who knew him, knew how important his family was.

What I will tell you is that my dad taught us what hard work and integrity looked like.

We had no idea how brave our parents were until we grew up and had families of our own. My parents traveled across country three times with five kids... in a car, not an RV. Having raised six kids with my husband, I'm not sure I would have done the same, especially three times! I'm afraid I would have left some of my kids on the side of the road. Just saying...

The first time my father's company transferred him to Farmington, NM, we were all young. My two younger brothers hadn't even started school. My mother had only seen the "wild west" on TV. She had never been away from the East coast. We had just arrived in Farmington and were waiting in the car with my mom while my dad checked us into the motel. While he was inside, a huge dust devil, which looks like a small tornado, blew through town and scared some horses pulling a covered wagon. Just like out of the movies, this horse-drawn wagon was heading straight for our car. I think we all thought we were going to die. We had never seen anything like it and I'm sure my mother was wondering what she had gotten herself into. Fortunately, the horses made their way around our car leaving everyone intact.

We had a lot of new experiences and made some lifelong friends during the two years we lived in New Mexico. Then, my dad's company transferred him back to Maine. My parents were brave enough to drive across country a second time with five kids. I can only imagine the patience it took to endure the long days in the car listening to the continuous cries of "Are we there yet?" These trips lasted about a week.

There would eventually be another trip across country. After I graduated high school, my parents decided to join other family members in a move to Las Vegas. My parents drove one car, and my older sister and I shared the driving of the second car. I hadn't had my driver's license for long, and it had taken me three times to pass the driving test. Looking back, this may not have been a wise decision. Like I said, my parents were brave. My parents lived and worked in Las Vegas until my dad retired from real estate and returned to Maine.

The thing I will remember and love the most about my father is the way he loved and cared for my mother. He taught me how a man should treat a woman. He showed me what love looks like. He made such an impact on me that when I was a young wife and didn't feel I was being treated the way I saw my father treat my mother, I would frequently say to my husband, "My father would never say that to my mother!" I expected to be treated the way my father treated my mother. He set the bar high, and I thank him for that.

When my mother was dying, I was fortunate to witness a tender moment between my parents. My mom was in a medicated state and my dad was stroking her face. I was standing next to him when he said, "How can she be dying? How can she be so sick? Look at her, she is so beautiful."

I will never forget that moment nor the love I felt for my dad.

My father cared for my mother while she lived with cancer for fifteen years. As a cancer patient, I can tell you how hard that is… not just for the patient, but the caregiver as well. My siblings and I never worried about the care our mother received, because we knew our dad was there for her. We were blessed to have witnessed this beautiful love story.

Thank you, Dad, for teaching us what love looks like and for showing us how to care for someone you love.

When we are born, we are placed in a line. We have no idea how long that line is or when it will be our turn to be pulled out of that line. I was pulled out of line and only by the grace of God, my older sister, Jayme, and my husband, Joe, was I able to get back in that line. What I learned from this experience is, that the things we think are so important—what we look like, the clothes we wear, the titles we carry, the houses we live in or the cars we drive—in the end, do not matter. What does matter most, is how we lived and how we loved.

RIP Dad

As I FINISHED READING the eulogy and walked away from the podium, my brother, Jim, stepped out from his pew and gave me the biggest hug I have ever received from him. We were both crying, and I could feel his love for me.

Following the church service, my siblings and I headed out to sea on a refurbished lobster boat to inter my dad's ashes. He was a practicing Catholic, so his urn was dropped over the side of the boat. According to the church, his ashes needed to stay together and not be scattered. To be honest, I was dreading this part of the ceremony. But to my surprise, the three hours on the boat with my siblings will always be a cherished memory. It was something I didn't realize I needed. There is just something about the sea air and the salt water that makes me so calm. I can hear the seagulls flying above just thinking of our time spent on the ocean.

Goodbye Dad

Later in the day, our entire family gathered at a nearby state park to honor our parents with a catered lobster feast. I believe there were 23 of us who had traveled from out of town to attend the service. It was an afternoon filled with love and beautiful memories.

Afterwards, we migrated to a property my brother and his family had rented nearby. We continued to enjoy one another's company and share our childhood memories with the younger generation. They will soon be tasked with sharing the family history and stories with their children.

The last time there was so many of us together was a surprise party celebrating my mom's 70th birthday and my parents' 50th anniversary. Before my mother died, I had the opportunity to ask her about her favorite memory. She told me it was that surprise party. So much work had gone into getting everyone to Maine to pull off the surprise. Hearing that it was her favorite memory made it all worthwhile. My siblings and I were aware that the next time our family gathered like this, one of us would be missing.

As we traveled through my hometown during the remainder of our visit, childhood memories continued to surface. When we drove by the first house our family lived in, it appeared so small compared to my memory of it. It made me wonder how our family of seven lived in such a small space. It seemed funny that I don't ever recall feeling as though we were living in anything less than what we needed.

I believe this house was where my mother discovered my artistic ability. My youngest brother had a large stuffed animal that I admired. My grandparents had given it to him for Christmas. It was a large dog that sat up on its hind legs. It had an oversized cone-shaped hat as well. Nothing about it was realistic, but it was adorable. One day as I sat on the toilet, I happened to have something to write with. While I was taking care of my business, I drew an exact miniature copy of this stuffed animal. When my mother discovered it, instead of scolding me for drawing on the bathroom wall, she became the proud mom. She didn't scrub if off or paint over it. What she did do was bring in all the neighbors to show off my artwork. If she was a modern-day mother, I'm sure she would have posted it on Instagram.

I was in kindergarten and first grade while we lived in that house. My first-grade teacher's name was Mrs. Bourke. She was also the principal of our elementary school. It was common for me to get in trouble for talking in class. Once I completed my work, I would turn around and help the students behind me finish up so we could move on to something else. One day, the teacher had had enough of me and decided to put me in the office for a "time out." She left me in the office alone. I'm not sure where I found the courage, but I figured I would just go home if I couldn't be in class with the rest of the kids. I walked out of the school, crossed the street by myself and continued home. My mother was on the phone with my teacher as I walked in the door. I can't imagine what it was like being my mother because I have never feared authority.

The two boys who sat behind me in that first-grade class, were identical twins. No one could tell them apart. I discovered a way to identify them but wouldn't reveal my secret. One day I noticed the twins wore different shoes. By looking down at the twin's shoes, I could tell them apart. I enjoyed challenging my classmates to try to tell the twins apart. When they were wrong, I would correct them. "How can you tell them apart?" They would ask. I would respond arrogantly, "I just can."

There was a boy in our neighborhood who was in my class. He would frequently get beat up by other boys in the school. One day his mother called my mother and asked her if I would walk to and from school with her son because, when he was with me, the other boys would leave him alone. I guess they were afraid of me. This may have built the foundation that started my strong dislike for anyone who was a bully. Once I witness someone being bullied, all common sense leaves me, and I just react. As an adult, I have put myself in danger while coming to the rescue of someone being bullied. I don't recommend or encourage this. It can be dangerous.

Our first move to New Mexico occurred when I finished first grade. We would remain there for two years while I attended second and third grade. It was a whole new world for us living in the West. We have great memories of sitting on our rear block wall waiting for someone to ride their horse down the alley behind our house. We would politely ask if we could get a ride on their horse. Most of the time, they would give each of us a short ride. This is one of my fondest memories. The not-so-fond memories involved the discipline we received. My mother was very small, not even 5 feet tall. As we grew and got older, she had a difficult time disciplining us. She would keep track of all the things we did wrong during the day. When my father returned home from work each day, she would give him a laundry list of our bad behavior. Once my father got settled, we were lined up on the five chairs in front of the French doors that led into the back yard. We had to pull our pants down and face away from our dad and he would hit us with his belt. Each of us received a different number of strikes according to how "bad" we had been that day. Let's be honest, I usually received the worst of the belt strikes. It hurt so much that I often felt the need to pee my pants. One time I remember my younger brother, Jimmy, was getting hit with the belt when my father lost his grip of the buckle and it struck my little brother, leaving a bloody mark on his behind. I still remember his crying and will never forget seeing his wound. Today this type of discipline would be considered child abuse, but at the time, we thought everyone was punished this way. I'm sure my parents had been and that's how they learned to discipline us. I'm not sure if the physical punishment became less effective as we got older, or if my parents began to realize we weren't learning anything from being hit. Our punishments became more painful when we began losing privileges. The physical pain from a yardstick or hairbrush breaking on my behind only lasted for moments, but the pain of losing a privilege could last weeks.

New Mexico memories

When I was in the second grade, the teacher handed out a large piece of construction paper and instructed us all to draw an animal. She then left us alone in the classroom to complete the task. I loved to draw and quickly drew a dog. One of my classmates saw my drawing and asked me if I would draw her animal for her. It was my pleasure to fulfill her request. As I was drawing, more of my classmates started lining up at my desk waiting for their turn to watch me draw an animal of their choice. Looking back, I chuckle thinking of what went through my teacher's mind when she came back into the room and saw the long line next to my desk as I eagerly drew each classmate's requested animal. I didn't understand why the teacher

8

reprimanded me for doing the other student's work. In my young mind, I was just helping.

There was a girl in my class named Luanne, and we did not get along at all. She would constantly challenge me and start a physical fight. I never hit her first, but once she hit me, it was on. The teacher frequently had to pull us apart while we were rolling on the ground fighting. We were then placed on opposite ends of the school building while the other students were playing at recess. I didn't really care. I thought most of the other kids were stupid anyway. I'm pretty sure I spent more recesses in time out than playing with the other kids. Today, we both would probably be suspended. I'm sure I still wouldn't have cared.

My mother would often share memories of her own school days. She attended a Catholic school where the teachers were nuns. My mother's family was poor. There were five girls and one boy in her family. Every year, each student was supposed to sell Christmas cards to raise money for the school. My mother knew it would be a hardship for her parents to purchase the cards from each of their school-age kids, but she was too afraid to return to school with the unsold Christmas cards. Instead, she would walk to school with her siblings and as soon as they were out of sight, she would run home and hide under a bench on the screened-in porch. She did this every day for two months before her teacher asked her older sister if my mother was feeling better. My mom's sister didn't know what the nun was referring to. She said her sister walked to school with her every day. I don't remember how my grandmother found out that my mother wasn't going to school; it was either her sister or the teacher. The next day, my grandmother didn't go to work and saw where my mother had been hiding every day. She surprised my mother when she peeked under the bench and found her. My mother was upset and told her why she was afraid to go to school. My grandmother was extremely angry at the school for instilling that type of fear in a child. She took my mother, walked her to school and gave the nun a piece of her mind. I'm pretty sure my grandparents never purchased the cards again.

When my mother was getting married, her parents worked for

the church. My grandfather was paid weekly, and the priests would put a portion of his check into a savings account for him. As a gift, the priests offered to pay for my mother's wedding. My parents married on Thanksgiving Day, the same as my grandparents. Because of the generosity of the church, my parents had a much nicer wedding than they could have imagined. It included a full sit-down Thanksgiving dinner. After their wedding, it was revealed that the church didn't pay for the wedding after all. They used my grandfather's entire savings to pay for it. My mother felt awful knowing that her wedding cost her parents their savings. This story and the fear my mother felt regarding the Christmas cards created a mistrust in me toward the priests and nuns I would encounter while attending church or Sunday school during my childhood. In fact, I hated going to catechism. While I was preparing for my confirmation, I had to go to confession. It's always been difficult for me to understand the need for confession. The church taught us that God knew all. He could see everything we did. So, when I was told I had to go into this little room and confess my sins, I didn't follow the logic of it all. God already knew what I did. Why did I need to tell a priest? When it came time for my confession, I was full of anxiety. I didn't want to tell anyone my sins, so I just made some stuff up. I guess I was committing another sin (lying) while confessing. I didn't care. God already knew. I was given some Hail Marys and Our Fathers to say and went on my way.

My parents on their wedding day

As I GOT OLDER, my father would drive us to catechism. I would get out of the car and walk down the walkway as my dad drove off. Then, I would sneak across the street and hang out at the library until it was time for him to pick us up. Cautiously, I would head back to the church and wait on the sidewalk. I'm pretty sure he never knew, or at least he didn't let on if he did. I'm probably going to hell.

Another childhood memory in Maine is probably our family's most overshared story. We did not go on a lot of vacations when we were younger. As a parent, I can only imagine the expense and the logistics involved in taking a family of seven on a trip.

This vacation involved a small, and I mean small, pull-behind trailer. I'm not even sure how the seven of us fit inside. It did not have an indoor bathroom or shower. We would use the nearby outhouses at the campground. When we brushed our teeth, the five of us would walk around with a paper cup and our toothbrush. We would brush our teeth, rinse with the water in the cup and spit out onto the ground. You might call it roughing it, but we would tell you it was fun.

One night during our vacation, after we had all gone to bed, one by one we had the need to use the bathroom. It was dark outside and there was no way we were going to walk to the outhouse. My parents had a port-a-potty set up in the middle of the trailer. It was basically a plastic bag draped over a stand with a toilet seat on top. I was one of the first to wake and use the port-a-potty, followed by my younger sister and then the older of my two brothers. As you can imagine, the plastic bag was getting full. By the time my older sister needed to go, the bag was full, and my parents told her to go to the bottom of the steps of the trailer and squat. She was a bit hesitant, but she complied.

Finally, the youngest, who had just been potty trained, woke up in a panic. He was doing a little dance as he told my parents he needed to use the bathroom. In their slumber, they told him to stand at the top of the stairs and pee. He no sooner started to pee when my older sister let out a scream that woke the entire campground. Lights came on in all the campers around us. I think they thought there might be a bear in the area. We were in Vermont after all.

My baby brother was so startled by my sister's scream that he started to cry. My barely awake parents were now trying to clean up and calm down my siblings. While that was happening, the rest of us realized what was going on and began to laugh uncontrollably. The more the three of us laughed, the more the other two cried. My parents scolded us for laughing as they tried to console the other two. Eventually, my parents were able to calm everyone down and get us all back to bed. You might think that was the end of it, but it wasn't. Every time it would get quiet, one of the three of us would start to giggle again, setting off the uncontrollable laughing followed by the crying. I don't remember how long it took to finally get us back to sleep.

This story has been told and retold almost every time our family has gotten together over the years. Initially, the two involved would be embarrassed and get mad at us for bringing it up. As they got older, I think they began to realize the humor in the situation.

Shortly before my mother passed away, I just had to ask her about the memory. I said to her, "Mom, tell me the truth. Were you and dad laughing too?" She smiled at me and nodded. As a parent, I know I would have had a hard time holding back my laughter as I was trying to calm down and clean up my kids.

It's our family's most priceless memory and I hope it continues to be shared for generations to come.

Camping in Vermont

THE NEXT HOUSE my parents owned would be just a few blocks up the street. My dad and his business partner had purchased some land and built a small subdivision with custom homes. That house was much bigger in comparison to the previous houses we had lived in. The street was also named after us. I'm not going to lie; that was cool. It is even more significant today since my parents are gone. It keeps their legacy alive. It makes me happy to know my children, their children and generations to come can visit and stand next to the street sign with family history. I hope they share some of the unforgettable memories that came with that house.

Whitworth Drive

The first night we slept in that new home, excitement and curiosity got the best of us. One of the features in the house was a laundry chute. It was just a cabinet door in our bathroom that, when opened, provided a view of the laundry room on the lower level. Of course, we needed to give this chute a try. The older of my two brothers climbed into the cabinet and dropped into the chute coming out in the laundry room. It seemed easy, so my younger sister, who was very petite, went next. I knew I was too big to fit, so I didn't even attempt to climb in. My stocky baby brother was sure he could do it—until he got stuck. He began to panic and cry. We tried to calm him down and get him loose, but nothing worked. You can only imagine the fear we felt as we tiptoed into my parent's bedroom to wake them up. Both my parents came flying out of bed not knowing what they were going to find or how serious the situation was. Fortunately, the fire department did not need to be called. My dad was able to maneuver my brother out of the tight space. I'm sure there were moments he believed he would need a saw. We were all disciplined and scolded enough so that we never tried it again. As a parent, I know my parents had to have a good laugh about this more than once. We all have.

Not long after we moved into that house, I remember feeling euphorically happy. I mean the kind of happy that you feel throughout your entire body. We were living in this custom-built home, and everything seemed so right. I was standing in our kitchen with my parents, when we heard the older of my two brothers' bloodcurdling scream coming from outside. We jumped up and ran outside to find my brother, Jimmy, hysterically screaming and crying. My parents were having a hard time understanding what he was trying to tell us. Finally, they were able to figure out that my baby brother, Joey, had been run over by a car. As soon as we knew what he was saying, we all headed toward the street. My brother continued screaming as he directed us to the long driveway that ran alongside the property next to our home.

My two brothers had been "helping" the old man who lived in the house rake his leaves. What they were doing was taking turns rolling down the driveway inside a trash can. They were being little boys and having a blast. The old man heard a car coming down the driveway and started waving his arms to get the driver's attention. Joey had just climbed out of the trash can and tried to get out of the way, but he tripped over his shoelace and fell. The car was pulling a flatbed trailer with another car on top of it. When the car stopped, Joey's small body was stuck between the two tires of the flatbed trailer. It was as if he had been run over by two cars. I'll never forget seeing his royal blue sweater sticking out from between those two tires.

My parents told my sisters and I to run and get help from the neighbors. We ran down the street screaming for help as loud as we could. The neighbors and my father were able to lift the trailer enough to slide my brother out before paramedics or police arrived. This most likely helped save his life. He was taken by ambulance to the hospital. One of our local police officers, Ronnie Costigan, rode with Joey in the back of the ambulance. During the ride, Officer Costigan kept Joey awake. He kept talking to him so he wouldn't slip into a coma before getting to the hospital. My parents recognized the part this special officer had in making sure Joey had the best chance for survival. When Joey arrived at the hospital, the doctors found he had suffered a broken femur, broken hip, every rib broken and two collapsed lungs. After the doctors did everything they could, they told my parents it was out of their hands. He spent the next two weeks in intensive care.

Our parents had no idea if he would survive. If he did, it was unknown if he would suffer any disabilities because of his injuries. My brother was very lucky. He did survive without any major issues. When he was finally released, he was still in a cast for his broken leg, and the whites of his eyes were completely red. The pressure from the trailer and car being on top of his little body, caused all the blood vessels in his eyes to burst. He was given crutches with wrist cuffs since he was unable to use regular crutches under his arms because of his broken ribs. He was afraid to use his crutches because he thought he was going to fall. Other than my father, who was at work all day, I was the only one big or strong enough to help my brother get around the house. I figured out that I could drag him around the house sitting on a blanket or bed sheet. Our house was two stories with the kitchen and bedrooms on the upper level and our family room and TV on the lower level. When my brother needed to go downstairs, I would sit on the top step, and he would scoot up behind me so I could grab his legs and carry him down the stairs piggyback style. This way I wouldn't crush his broken ribs by trying to carry him. I taught him how to go up the stairs one step at a time by sitting on the bottom step and using his good leg to push himself up. At night I would sleep on the floor next to his bed as he was unable to turn himself over without help due to his injuries. When he wanted to turn over, I would gently roll him and then go back to sleep until he needed my help again. His accident and recovery created a strong bond between the two of us.

When we returned to school following Joey's accident, it was a bit uncomfortable. Walking into my 5th-grade classroom, I was nervous and smiling because everyone was looking at me. We had been out of school for about two weeks while my brother was in intensive care. As I walked to my desk, one of the boys in the class yelled out, "Look at her, she's smiling! Her little brother was run over by a car and she's smiling!" I was so embarrassed by his outburst that I started to cry. The teacher scolded him, but the damage was done. I would later find out that the boy who yelled out the hurtful comment had been run over by a car himself. He had been dragged quite a distance and needed to have a plate put in his head from his injuries. When I found this out, I think I realized his inappropriate outburst was probably a result of memories of his own injuries.

We were all changed by this accident. I became extremely anxious any time I would start to feel happy. Happiness was always associated with anxiety as I waited for the next horrible thing to happen. I know there have been times in my life when I sabotaged my own happiness, believing I would then be in control of the next bad thing that was going to happen in my life. It has taken a lot of work and a lot of time to learn to enjoy just being happy without "fear" attached to it.

Recently I learned that unhealed childhood trauma manifests as:
- fixing others
- people pleasing
- codependency
- external validation
- living on high alert
- fear of abandonment
- deprioritizing your own needs
- a need to prove yourself
- tolerating abusive behavior
- attracting narcissistic partners
- difficulty setting boundaries

It's easy to look back on my life and recognize how all of the above surfaced in our family members' lives. Each of us experienced at least one symptom but probably had no idea why.

During the last week of school, while I was in sixth grade, I managed to break my arm. The weather was beautiful, and our class was outside playing kickball for PE class. After kicking the ball, I ran as fast as I could towards first base. My feet were going faster than my brain and I tumbled and rolled over first base. The teacher quickly came over to see if I was all right. It was obvious my arm was broken. My teacher gently supported my arm as we walked toward the school to call my parents. As we walked away, I heard one of my classmates yell, "She was safe, right?"

My father came to pick me up and took me to the ER. We sat there for four hours before they called me back. I was given some anesthesia to knock me out while they set my arm. The doctor told me to count backwards from 100. One of the doctors working on me must have been doing his residency because I could hear the other doctor instructing him on how to set my arm. As he pulled on my wrist, I could hear the bones cracking as he released it. While this was happening, I arched my back from the pain. After my cast was put on, the doctor sat me up and told me he was going to help me off the gurney. Instead of him helping me, I jumped off. When I did this, the two doctors looked at one another and realized the anesthesia did not work. The doctor walked me out to my father and told him I had a very high tolerance for pain. I spent most of that summer with a cast on my arm.

When I was in junior high, or middle school as they call it today, I became interested in becoming a majorette. My best friend at the time and I happened to walk by the auditorium during a meeting for those interested, and we stopped in. We were bored, so we decided to try out. The only problem was I had never twirled a baton. I can't remember if my friend had. We were taught a short routine that we would need to perform for tryouts. Although I didn't know what I was doing, I was excited. That night I spent hours twirling a broom in the garage. I was twirling a broom, which is a skill. A couple of days later, I walked to our nearest dime store (I'm sure it's the equiv- alent to the Dollar Store today) and purchased a baton for two dollars. I felt official. Every night I would practice until the day came for tryouts. There were two other girls trying out who knew how to twirl. They gave instruction to the younger kids at the recreation center. I didn't let their experience scare me. I performed my routine to the best of my ability and was surprised to be chosen as one of the two to make the squad. We were seventh graders, and we were the alternates to the squad. The idea was to teach us the routines and have us available to fill in if one of the older girls couldn't perform. It made me feel rather accomplished to have succeeded the first time I tried.

The following year, we all needed to try out again to create the regular squad. The older girls had moved on to high school, and it was our turn to "Carrie On". My best friend and I both made the squad again. After selection, we had to try out again to see who head majorette would be. Everyone was convinced that one of the more experienced girls would get the position. I didn't let that keep me from doing the best I could. Somehow, I outperformed the rest and was chosen to be head majorette. I don't think I ever realized what an accomplishment that was. I went from never twirling a baton to becoming head majorette in just a year. The sad part is, I don't ever recall my parents watching any of my performances.

The previous squad had ordered new uniforms, but they never had the chance to wear them because they weren't ready in time. Our squad would be the first to wear the uniforms. The girl who had previously been head majorette was very slender. All the uniforms had been made to their measurements. As soon as it was announced that I would be the new head majorette, the rest of the squad told me the uniform was never going to fit me. But, when I put my beautiful uniform on, it fit perfectly! You would have thought they used my measurements to make it. The sleeves were perfect. The length was perfect. It was amazing. All the other girls needed to have their uniforms altered for a proper fit. I was the only one who didn't need any alterations. To be honest, I was shocked that the uniform fit me as well as it did. I should have realized that my body image did not match reality. I still sometimes struggle with that today.

I STARTED PLAYING tennis while I was in middle school. Loving the sport, I played every day during the summer for three years. I would ride my bike or walk to the tennis courts. Spending hours hitting the ball against the backstop on the court, I built up my strength and accuracy. It was fun to play against different boys and I enjoyed it when I beat them. My mother used to tell me that if I kept on beating them, they wouldn't play with me anymore. My response would always be, I wasn't going to let them beat me and I didn't care if they didn't want to play against me. I regularly played in tournaments during the summer and loved it. One day my father showed up and was sitting in his car watching me play. I was so excited to see him watching me. It was the first time. He drove me home when I was finished and all I wanted to hear him say was that I had played well. Instead, he told me how I could have done better. I was crushed and didn't take his criticism to heart since I had never seen him play tennis. Not long after that, I stopped playing tennis. I remember hearing my mother telling people about my tennis. She bragged about how well I played. Her stories always ended with, "Carrie played tennis until she discovered boys, and then she quit." I never had the heart to tell her the reason I quit playing tennis was because she never came to watch me play.

It was the summer before ninth grade when I met a new neighbor who would ultimately become my best friend. We got off to a rocky start, and the friendship almost never happened. A neighbor told a friend and I that there was a girl our age in the family. We decided to go introduce ourselves. We knocked on the door and waited. When the door opened, we were met by Marcia. We told her who we were and welcomed her to the neighborhood. As our conversation concluded, we told Marcia that we would be playing tennis the next day and invited her to join us. My girlfriend and I looked forward to meeting up with her the next day. We went to the tennis courts where we always played and kept our eye out for our new friend. She never showed up and we figured she didn't really like us and didn't want to play. The summer went by, and we didn't see her until school started. When we saw Marcia in school, we weren't sure what to say. I don't remember how the conversation started, but we all were confused about why we hadn't met up at the tennis courts. It never dawned on us that we forgot to mention which tennis courts. My girlfriend and I always played at the high school courts, but Marcia went to the junior high courts. I'm sure when we didn't show up, she probably thought we were the mean girls. I am forever grateful that we figured it out and didn't let a misunderstanding keep us from starting a friendship that continues to this day. We don't get to see each other as often as we like, but when we do get together, it's like we just saw each other yesterday. We may be 3,000 miles apart, but if I need her, she'll be there for me and vice versa.

Myself and my BFF, Marcia

ONE OF MY biggest milestones happened just a couple of months before my parents sold that house. I graduated high school and attended my senior prom. I had been looking forward to this event throughout my high school years. It would be the first time in my life that all the focus would be on me. Our high school did not have junior proms or girl's reverse or any other type of formal dances, so our senior prom was a big deal. Only seniors and their dates were allowed to attend. My excitement and anticipation were short lived when I found out my parents were going to let my younger sister go to MY prom because her boyfriend was in my class. I cried and begged my parents not to let her go to my prom. This was my moment, and she was taking it away from me. This only reenforced my feelings that I didn't matter. I don't think my parents ever realized how devastated I was to have this one moment that was supposed to be all about me taken away.

My senior picture

CHAPTER 2

*O*ur old home takes me back to a high school memory. I had taken a short cut that many of us took through the woods. This day, an older boy passed me on the path. It made me nervous so after a few moments, I took a quick look back in his direction. He was looking down and had his penis out of his pants and in his hand. Once I saw this, I immediately started running. Since I was wearing chunky heels and a skirt, I tripped and fell dropping all my books and my purse. Quickly, I got up and took off running, leaving all my possessions behind. Finally, I made it to my neighborhood and felt better with houses around but continued to run until I made it home. When I got there, no one was home, and all the doors were unlocked as they often were. As I ran through the house, my heart was pounding. I hurried to lock all the doors, and then continued to pace while looking out the windows to make sure he hadn't followed me. When my mother got home, I told her what happened, and she called the police. From the description I gave, they believed it may have been an older brother of a girl who attended our high school. The police said he had attempted to rape his sister earlier in the week. One of our neighbors found my belongings and returned them to me. There is no doubt I had a guardian angel watching over me that day. That was the last time I walked home alone through the woods.

The first time I ever tried marijuana was in those woods. About 10 girlfriends and I were walking together to our high school to watch our football team play for the state championship. My friends didn't realize I was just excited to be included in the group. We came to a clearing, and unbeknownst to me, we were going to smoke some pot. I had never tried it before; I think I was the only one who hadn't. We sat in a large circle and passed joints and pipes around as we each took hits from them. All my friends were saying how stoned they were, but I felt nothing, so I kept on taking more and more hits. Still, I felt nothing. I was beginning to think, "What's the big deal?" We all stood up and started walking towards the high school again. That's when it hit me. Suddenly it felt as though I was in a dream; then it felt like I was floating. I kept pinching myself to make sure I was still there. I'm sure it was quite comical. We arrived at the game, and we were all stoned. While walking past the stands, I heard my name called. Looking up, I saw my father and froze. I was positive he could tell I was high. Forcing a smile, I waved at him as I kept walking with my friends. His presence scared me straight and my high was short lived.

In another nearby wooded area, that was called "Jakes," I managed to break a front tooth. My parents had joined a bowling league and went out every Friday night. This was an opportunity for me to go drinking with my friends. I was not allowed to go to Jakes, but it was where all the cool kids hung out. Every Monday at school I would hear about the parties other kids attended and a lot of them were at Jakes. I told my parents I was going to my girlfriend's house. What we did was stand outside the corner store and asked people going in to buy us some wine. I had never drunk wine before, but it sounded like a good idea. It didn't take long before someone took us up on our offer. They came out with some Boone's Farm wine, enough for us to share. The girl who was supposed to share with me didn't like it, so I drank the entire bottle myself. After we got our wine, we headed to Jakes. It was wintertime and the small pond in the center of the wooded area was frozen over. I eventually laid down on the upper embankment surrounding the pond. I could hear everyone but felt as though I really wasn't there. Some guy friends from school showed up and started goofing off. One of them came over and rolled me down the embankment on to the pond. When I hit the ice on the pond, I broke my front tooth. I started crying and saying that the boys weren't going to like me anymore because of my tooth. The tooth didn't fall out, it just got pushed back so it didn't look like it was there any longer. Now, I had to go home and figure out what I was going to tell my parents. When I arrived home, my parents were still out with their bowling league. I figured it would probably be a good idea to go to bed so they couldn't tell I had been drinking. I made up some lie about tripping on a crack in the sidewalk and they seemed to buy it. My mother took me to an orthodontist to see what they could do. The orthodontist stuck his finger in my mouth to see how loose my tooth was. Without any warning, he pulled the tooth forward. I was so mad, and it hurt so much that I bit him. He yelled at me and said, "You bit me!" I told him, "Well you shouldn't have pulled my tooth without telling me first." He stabilized my tooth with some temporary braces. Initially, this solved the problem. Eventually, I would need a root canal. Years later, the rod for the root canal broke and my tooth was slowly falling out. I ended up having about $10,000 worth of dental work on that tooth. I'm guessing God was sending me a message.

During my senior year in high school, I may have attended about half my classes. There was a morning I needed a note from my mother so I could be excused to go to the dentist. When I went into her bedroom to ask her to write the note, she was still in bed and tired. Knowing I could write like her, she told me to write the note myself. That opened an opportunity for me. I wrote the note and was excused. Since it worked once, why wouldn't it work again? After that, I began writing notes every week, choosing different classes to be excused from each time. My boyfriend and I repeatedly ditched school and never got caught. Today, we could never get away with it because of the stricter attendance policies.

Knowing how difficult it was for me to stay focused my senior year, I supported all my kids graduating before they were 18. My oldest started school when she was only four so that wasn't a problem for her. My second earned enough extra credits to graduate a year early with honors. My third graduated six months early, and my youngest graduated 18 months early with high honors. As a parent, it was a sense of relief to have them all graduate before they experienced the "senioritis" I suffered from.

My boyfriend was the captain of the swim team. When he was in junior high school, he went to a swim team tryout even though he did not know how to swim. I guess this was like me trying out to be a majorette without knowing how to twirl a baton. The coach must have been a great guy, because he taught him how to swim. And like me, he went on to become team captain. At the end of the year there was a team party at a camp on the lake. There were no adults, so of course there was booze and pot. My boyfriend had never tried smoking pot and I had my one experience. Still, I encouraged him to try it. He did and proceeded to get high.

While we were at the party, it snowed. When it was time for us to leave, the ground was completely white. The snowplow had not come by yet, so it was almost impossible to see the road. My boyfriend was high, and I was scared to death as he tried to navigate his way home. We had never been so afraid in our lives. I realize everything was amplified because he was stoned, and I just knew we were going to die. Thank goodness there wasn't any traffic, so we didn't have to worry about getting hit head on. It would have been nice if someone was ahead of us though. Their tire tracks would have shown us where the road was. We couldn't just pull over and wait for the plow or another car to come by because I had a curfew. That drive home kept us from ever getting high again. It's a miracle that we didn't die or kill someone else. Maybe it was God's plan to scare us straight.

Once my younger siblings and I were aware that we would be moving and leaving behind the street named after our family, we decided we had to take the street sign. Without our parent's knowledge, we took a cardboard sign, that read "Sesame Street" from my brothers' bedroom. While no one was looking, I stood at the base of the existing street sign and had my brothers and younger sister climb on my shoulders until they could reach the sign. They removed the original sign with our name on it and replaced it with the cardboard sign. We then hid the street sign so we could later pack it in our belongings. As you can see by the newspaper clipping dated 6/2/76, the "vandalism" caught a newspaper reporter's attention. The little blurb says that the sign was painted. Trust me, there was no paint involved. Apparently, my parents found some humor in the whole thing because this clipping was found among their keepsakes. Since we were all juveniles, I think we are safe from prosecution. Besides, the statute of limitations has probably run out.

One of the things that was unique about our neighborhood was a home that housed mentally challenged adults. A lot of them had Down syndrome. The home was called "the funny farm." I don't know who created the name, but I just remember that was what we called it. As time passed and people became more aware, the home eventually became The Noyes Home. That was the last name of the original owner. I believe he started the home for his son who was mentally challenged.

One of the residents was a man named Freddy. He was about 50 years old and was more highly functioning than most of the other residents. Freddy was allowed to ride his bike throughout our small town and was known by most of the local citizens. Our police department enjoyed Freddy. They gave him a retired uniform to wear around town as he rode his bike. No one thought about liability at the time. He was so proud to ride around wearing it. One day Freddy was at an intersection talking to a friend of ours. While they were standing there, a car pulled up beside them, and the occupants tried to get directions from Freddy. They were obviously not from the area and assumed Freddy was a police officer. When Freddy couldn't help them, they became insistent and pushed him for more information. Freddy became more uncomfortable, pulled out his toy gun and told them to leave him alone or he was going to shoot them. Not understanding or believing what was happening, they took off. I believe they called our police department to report this "officer." Unfortunately for Freddy, his retired uniform had to be returned. It's a miracle that something worse didn't happen.

Living in a neighborhood with a home for the mentally challenged helped us to be comfortable around people with disabilities. We knew many of the residents' names, and we would wave and say hello to them as we walked to and from school every day. Little did I know that these experiences were preparing me for my future.

CHAPTER 3

efore Joe and I headed home from Maine, we had the opportunity to take a drive and visit a cousin I had reconnected with via social media. He and his wife live in New Hampshire on the same pond where we lived when I was just a toddler. While there, I was able to show Joe the first house my parents purchased for about $5,000. The house was also on the pond where my mother and I almost drowned. My grandparents (father's parents) lived on the pond as well, and their house, which was across the small dirt road from us, had a beach. One day, with both my father and grandfather at work, we were spending the afternoon at my grandparent's small sandy beach. My grandmother could not swim, and neither could my mother. My younger sister had just been born and I was a year old. Somehow, I managed to toddle into the water and began floating away before my mother could get to me. The small beach lead into the pond. The first few feet were shallow; then there was a large drop off. My mother told me she was standing on the edge of that drop off, on the tip of her toes, reaching for me. She was able to grab me by my big toe and pull me back in. If she had taken one more step, she would have been over her head in the water and both of us would likely have drowned.

When I think of this story, it makes me think how many lives would be so different today. There are many members of our family who wouldn't be here. My two brothers would not have been born and their families wouldn't exist. Of course, my children and their children also wouldn't have been born. Apparently, God wanted us all here and, for that, I am extremely grateful.

The first house my parents purchased

My father shared another incident that almost prevented this book and all the memories in it. When he was a teenager, he was being mischievous with his best friend. Together they were able to hoist a large boulder to the top of an old bridge. They waited until they saw a car coming and thought it would be a good idea to scare someone by dropping the boulder on the car. It just so happens that the car was a police patrol car. The two of them pushed the boulder off, and it landed right on top of the engine as it drove across the bridge. A few more inches and it would have landed on the roof of the police vehicle, possibly injuring or killing the police officer. They took off and were lucky not to be caught. I shake my head when I share this story, because my father could have gone to jail for being stupid and, again, none of us would have ever existed.

Another story my mother shared with me was about her father's brother. When she was growing up, it was known that her father's brother (her uncle) was impotent. Despite this knowledge, her uncle and his wife had two sons. My mother and her siblings often wondered how that was possible. It just so happens that the youngest sister was home one day when she saw her father and her aunt walking down the stairs in their home. The only rooms upstairs were bedrooms. I guess that's how they handled infertility before the treatments that are available today. This story led my mother and her siblings to question whether their two cousins were their half-brothers, but they never asked their parents. They kept their conclusions to themselves.

It appears, though, that their speculation may have some merit. Several of our family members have done DNA ancestry tests. We have come up with some second cousin matches that we didn't know existed. I grew up knowing all my cousins, or at least I thought I did. One day I may be contacted by one of these second cousins, and I will share this story. I hope they find it as amusing as I do.

Although the purpose of this trip was not something any of us looked forward to, I believe we all managed to create some lasting memories. As we boarded the plane to head home, my head was filled with many emotions once again. I was leaving my hometown and many childhood memories. We had no idea when we would return but realized that the next trip would be different in so many ways. On one hand, the reasons and the people for whom we normally go "home" to visit will no longer be there. On the other hand, we will get to visit people we normally don't have the luxury to spend time with. We will have the opportunity to see areas of the state outside where I grew up. It won't be better or worse, just different. Change is good... right? Only time will tell.

Our plane landed and we were back home where we have lived our entire 32 years of marriage. Neither of us has ever really loved Las Vegas: it has just been an easy place to make a living and raise our family. Now that our family is grown and retirement is near, we are excited to see what lies ahead for us.

CHAPTER 4

I had just graduated high school when my parents decided to move across country and join family in Las Vegas. On our trip, we drove two vehicles approximately 3,000 miles. As I mentioned in my father's eulogy, my parents and brothers rode in one car, and my older sister Jayme and I shared the driving in the second car. Somehow, we made it without any accidents. The scariest part of the trip for me was driving through Chicago. It happened to be rush hour traffic. There also was heavy construction going on, and the lanes on the highway were not clear. Temporary lines were everywhere and were very confusing to a new driver. I was gripping the steering wheel tightly; my knuckles were white. As I was following my dad, it was necessary to stay close, so no one would get between us. If I lost sight of his car, I would have no idea which way to go. We didn't have cell phones to keep in touch, only CB radios. I was relieved once we made it through Chicago and I have never had a desire to return.

Our trip was not without family shenanigans. At one point, we stopped at a rest area to stretch our legs and use the restroom. Initially, I stayed behind. But, while waiting for the others, my bladder told me I should probably go ahead and take a bathroom break. As I entered the lady's restroom and went into a stall, I looked down and recognized Jayme's shoes on the feet in the stall next to me. I couldn't help myself. With a big smile on my face, I reached down and grabbed her ankle. Hearing her gasp gave me a great sense of pride. You could tell she wanted to scream but was holding back. She was in sheer panic mode before she recognized the ring on my hand. To say she was mad is an understatement. Yes, it was evil, but also very amusing… at least for me. No wonder we always struggled to get along.

Once we arrived in Las Vegas, my boyfriend, who had made the trip with us, entered the Navy and began bootcamp. After he left, I figured I would get a job since I had no intention of going to college. I walked across a vacant lot to the nearest grocery store and asked the manager if they were hiring. He had me fill out an application and gave me a job as a checker. My first day on the job, I met the best-looking guy I had ever seen. His name was Joe. He was one of the courtesy clerks working at the store. He had the most beautiful black curly hair and gorgeous green eyes. I couldn't take my eyes off him. Every time we worked with one another; I would go home with sore cheeks because he made me smile so much. I'd be lying if I told you I didn't have a crush on him, but the little voices in my head were telling me I had no chance.

Best looking guy I have ever met

I STILL HAD my Navy boyfriend, but all Joe would have had to do was ask, and he would have become my new boyfriend. It never happened, and I convinced myself that it was because I wasn't pretty or thin enough. So, when my boyfriend returned home from boot-camp and asked me to marry him, I accepted. The little voices in my head told me that I might as well marry him, because I didn't know if anyone else would ask me.

My now fiancé came to visit during Christmas. While he was visiting, we told my parents we were going to the movies. Instead, we rented a motel room for a few hours. While there, we talked about having a baby.

The following month, we found out we did, in fact, make a baby. My parents had just purchased a house, and it needed some work before they could move in. The entire interior had to be painted and the flooring replaced. I was expected to help, but morning sickness was starting to set in. All I could do was lie on the sofa while my mother prepared to move.

It wasn't difficult to tell when my mother was upset because she would start to hum. As I was lying on the sofa, my mother was coming in and out of the room humming. I knew I had to tell her I was pregnant. Taking a deep breath, I began by saying, "Mom." She stopped and responded curtly with, "What?" There was no turning back; now I had to tell her. Nervously, I told her I thought I knew why I wasn't feeling well. Looking back, I don't know how I got the words out. She asked me if I was sure and told me I would have to tell my father. Filled with anxiety over that thought, I had no idea how I would say it out loud again. My father came home for lunch and, fortunately for me, my mother filled him in. I'm pretty sure he cried. Once the reality set in, my parents wanted to know our plans. I was in disbelief when my father suggested an abortion as a solution. This was something I never thought I would hear coming from him. He was and has always been a practicing Catholic. I made it clear that an abortion was not an option. I was already engaged, and we would be getting married soon. We started making plans for a "quickie wedding" that would take place the next month.

One of the hardest things about finding out I was pregnant was telling my older sister. She had undergone some needed surgery that resulted in her losing her ability to ever have kids. I was 18 and she had just turned 20. She had come to Vegas from Maine to recover from her surgery. I cannot imagine what she experienced when she found out her younger sister was having a baby, while knowing that she would never have one. It was just one more reason for her to resent me.

After our wedding, I continued to live with my parents while my new husband finished electronics school in the Navy. He finished top of his class and was able to choose where he wanted to be stationed. He decided on Norfolk, VA. The plan was for me to join him, and we would embark on a new journey. Neither of us had ever lived on our own. Together, we purchased our first vehicle—a forest green 1972 four-door Ford Gran Torino. Discovering adulthood, we had fun exploring this new Navy town and finding our first one-bedroom apartment across the street from the ocean. Unfortunately, due to our ignorance, we moved into an area with high drug and prostitution traffic. We would sit on the back steps of the apartment complex and count how many times the hookers would get picked up and dropped off… mostly by sailors.

We started our new life together while waiting for the birth of our daughter. One day, when I was about eight months pregnant, we were standing in line at the grocery store. I happened to look at a candy bar and suddenly had a craving for one. It was 25 cents at the time, and we were writing a check for our groceries. I made the mistake of asking my husband for permission to purchase the candy bar, which he refused to give. I was crushed—not because I couldn't have the candy bar, but because I felt like I wasn't worth 25 cents to my husband. This simple request and his response damaged our relationship.

While sleeping one night, I was awakened by what felt like I was wetting the bed. Jumping up, I quickly headed to the bathroom. Each time I took a step, I could hear splashing on the floor. My water had broken. The baby was about a week early. We called the doctor and he told us to head to the hospital. The naval hospital was full, so we went to the nearest private Catholic hospital. I was so embarrassed because my pants where wet and I was afraid anyone who saw me would think I peed my pants. I didn't think about the fact that I was nine months pregnant and if someone saw me, they would be able to figure out my water had broken.

We arrived at the hospital, and I was wheeled to my room. As we reached the labor and delivery floor, I could hear women yelling in pain from their contractions. My initial contractions were relatively mild, and I thought these women were being overly dramatic. In less than an hour, my labor pains became more intense. With each contraction, I began to yell. As the contractions grew in intensity, I got louder and may have included a few cuss words. A nurse came into my room and asked me to quiet down because I was scaring the other women. I totally ignored the request, because I could hear the other women crying out in pain as well. The nurse left my room, I had another contraction and my yelling continued. My husband kept telling me to quiet down. I looked at him with the devil in my eyes and told him he had better shut up or I was going to call the nurse and have her kick him out of my room. He was smart enough to just sit there quietly throughout the remainder of my labor. My husband was squeamish and told me he would not be going into the delivery room. I lost so much respect for him that day. I thought he was a total puss. I was going to push a little human out of my body, and he couldn't even be by my side for support because he was too squeamish? My labor progressed quickly, especially for my first delivery. I refused drugs and wanted a natural delivery. After three and a half hours, I delivered my 8 lb., 5 oz. daughter without my husband by my side. She was absolutely beautiful, and I was so in love with her. My dream had come true… I was a mom!

Once our daughter was born, my husband began to struggle with all the attention she took away from him. Prior to her birth, I would get up every morning and make him breakfast before he went to work. After getting up multiple times during the night to feed her, I did not have the energy to wake up early to make his breakfast. It became obvious that he resented this. This man needed to grow up and learn how to be not only a supportive husband, but a loving father as well.

I have always battled my weight and felt very insecure about my size. I had lost a lot of weight prior to getting pregnant. During my pregnancy, I worried constantly that I was going to become the size of a cow. Approximately six weeks following her birth, I tried on my size nine jeans and was pleasantly surprised that I could zip them up. I was standing in the mirror admiring my progress when my husband walked in. I proudly said, "Look, I can get my jeans on!" His response was, "You can still lose some weight."

Teen mom

I WAS DEVASTATED. With that one comment, he took the wind out of my sails. He made it clear how he saw me. After that, our sex life was ruined. Every time he wanted to be intimate, the little voices in my head reminded me how unattractive I was to him. Sex became a chore. His response regarding my weight haunted me and prevented me from ever enjoying sex with him again.

We had our second daughter 18 months after our first baby. She was almost identical to her sister. She was one ounce less at birth. I came home from the hospital and was sure to put their names on their pictures, because I didn't know if I would be able to tell them apart in the future.

Every morning my husband would get up early and go to work. He always locked our apartment door behind him. When I woke, I could usually hear my oldest daughter playing. One morning I woke to silence. Quickly, I got out of bed and found my front door open and my daughter was nowhere to be found. I was frantic. I had to make some decisions very quickly. I didn't know if I should call the police or just start looking for her. I made a difficult choice to leave my newborn alone in her crib while I looked for her sister. I pulled on a pair of jeans but didn't take the time to put on shoes even though it was cold outside. I didn't know which way to look first. We lived across the street from the ocean. Could she be walking on the beach? Behind our apartment building was a four-lane highway. Was she going to walk out into traffic? She was only 18 months old. She had never even walked down the concrete stairs that led to our second-floor apartment. I saw a lady across the street watering her plants and yelled, "Have you seen my baby?" She must have thought I was crazy. She shook her head. Since she hadn't seen my daughter, I headed to the parking lot behind our building. I was calling her name as loud as I could. Finally, I saw her walking in the parking lot. She was wearing a yellow Carter's onesie pajama—the kind with the feet in them. As soon as she saw me, she said, "Hi Mom!" I was so relieved. I never hugged her so tight. We hurried back to her little sister. From that day forward, whenever my husband went to work, I got up and latched the deadbolt that was out of reach for my little girl.

When it was time to have our second daughter baptized, we had to attend pre-baptism classes at the Catholic Church on the naval base. We met with Father Murphy (what else would his name be). The first question he asked us was, "Have you decided on a name?" I proudly responded, "Yes, her name is Casey Lee." He replied with, "Do you realize she has to live with that name?" I was understandably offended and upset with his response. I told him that my name was Carrie and he then replied, "And didn't everyone make fun of you growing up?" This angered me even more. I told him that I liked my name because no one else had it. I also told him my husband's name was Dana and my oldest daughter was Cortney. I explained how I liked all our names because they were unisex and on paper you couldn't tell whether we were male or female. I'm not even sure why I agreed to go forward with the baptism, but we did. This was just another experience that added to my distaste for the Catholic Church and why Joe and I refer to ourselves as recovering Catholics.

Before my husband's enlistment was up, I returned to Las Vegas with our two girls to get a job and buy a house while he was still employed by the Navy. I would be away from him for three months.

Fortunately, I was able to find a job at the nearest grocery store. They didn't have any checker positions available, so I was hired to work in the bakery. When I walked into the bakery on my first day, one of the employees said out loud, "Wait until the boss sees her." I was very naive and had no clue what they meant.

I was only 21 years old. My boss was 32 and from the Philippines. Initially he told me he was from Hawaii and lived with his business partner. I would later find out that his business partner was his ex-wife. It wasn't long before it became obvious that my boss was interested in me. He was very flirtatious and would come back to work after his shift if I was working. I'll be honest, I really didn't mind the attention. It was so much more than I had been getting from my husband.

While working and taking care of my two girls during those three months, I never missed my husband, not even for a minute. The time away made me realize how little I loved him. Shortly after he arrived in Las Vegas, I told him I wanted a divorce. My parents were furious with me. They encouraged me to seek counseling to save my marriage. I tried to explain that all the counseling in the world was not going to make me love my husband. The feelings were not there, and I wasn't sure they ever had been.

Not long after the divorce, I told my parents I was going to marry my boss from the bakery. They believed the only reason he wanted to marry me was to get his green card, but I ignored their warning. We were married shortly thereafter.

It seemed that as soon as I said, "I do," everything changed. It became clear he had taken advantage of my vulnerability and naiveté. He totally manipulated me, and it wasn't long before he became abusive to both the girls and me. A few months after we were married, I became pregnant with our son. During this time, we opened a bakery in the same shopping center where we had met. We needed to use my house as collateral to get the funding for the bakery. I knew my husband was an excellent baker, but I had no idea what a terrible businessman he was.

On our baby's due date, I woke with contractions. They were coming rather quickly, so I jumped in the shower. When I got out of the shower and I was drying off, my husband woke and asked me where I was going. He told me he needed to go open our bakery. I sarcastically asked him if he could drop me off at the hospital on his way. He reluctantly decided he should probably go to the hospital with me. Our initial plan was to drop my girls off at my parents' house before heading to the hospital. My parents' house was 20 minutes away, and my contractions were getting more frequent and stronger each time. I had to call to wake them and ask them to drive to our house to get the girls, because I knew we wouldn't make it to the hospital in time. As we waited outside for my parents, my contractions continued to increase with frequency and strength. We finally made the decision to take the girls to the hospital with us, because this baby was coming. As we started backing out of the driveway, my parents arrived. They quickly took the girls and we headed to the hospital, which, thankfully was only five minutes away.

As soon as we arrived at the ER, the nurses asked me how far apart my contractions were. "Thirty seconds," was my response. I was quickly admitted and prepared for delivery. When my doctor arrived, I told him if he would break my water, this baby would be born. The doctor asked me if he could put his gloves on first. I guess I was rushing him but, just like I said, as soon as he broke my water, the baby came right out. In about 90 minutes, from first contraction to his first breath, I delivered a 9 lb., 3 oz. baby boy. He was beautiful and I was in love with my first son. My husband came into our room and asked if he could go open our bakery now. Shaking my head, I told him to go. If he was more concerned about our business, than his wife and newborn son, then I didn't want him there anyway. Less than 24 hours later, I was home with my new baby. My husband told me if I wasn't coming home, he was going to bring the books from the bakery to the hospital. His level of compassion for me after giving birth showed me how little he cared for me.

After our son was born, his anger and rage became out of control. One day I was frightened that he might harm the girls, so I secretly opened my bedroom window in our small one-story home and lowered the girls to the ground. I told them to run to the neighbor's house and stay there. Later, as I tried to get out the front door, he came up behind me and slammed my head in the door jam. It caused me to see stars and fall to my knees. My head has a permanent indentation where the door hit me.

During this incident, my youngest brother Joey called, and I told him I needed help. He came as quickly as he could and immediately attacked my husband and threatened him should he ever touch me or the girls again. While my husband was lying on the floor, I walked over to him and took back my power. I kicked him as hard as I could right between his legs. I'm not proud of it, but that was the moment I began to become stronger and more independent.

After three years, we closed the bakery. We had to file bankruptcy, and we lost my home to foreclosure. We also had two cars repossessed. We lost everything we had. My husband couldn't find work in Vegas and went to California. I stayed behind with the kids and continued to live in my house while it went through the foreclosure process. He would come home on weekends and then head back to California. While this was happening, his ex-wife dropped his two teenage kids from the Philippines on my doorstep. They had been in this country for less than six months. I didn't know them, and they barely spoke English. It was a difficult and stressful time and added to our quickly deteriorating marriage.

A few years later, while we were still married and living together but no longer sharing the same bed, a friend of mine from high school came to town and got in touch with me. We planned to have dinner together. Nothing more, just old friends catching up with one another. I drove him to the airport following our dinner.

My husband could sense me pulling away and was attempting to be nice to me. He mentioned something about my working late. I told him I had driven a friend to the airport. He lost his mind when he realized it was a friend with whom I had a history. His oldest daughter was living with us at the time. He asked her if she knew what I was doing, (she did) but before she could answer, he hit her so hard on the side of her head that he knocked her onto the floor.

After I called 911, the police gave him the option of leaving the house or going to jail. He left the house. Today, he probably wouldn't have that option.

I knew I needed to get out of the marriage, but first I had to figure out how I would support my little family. I signed up for real estate school and got my license. Proudly, I became "Rookie of the Year" in our office. We divorced after six years of marriage, and I was a single mother of three working three jobs to make enough income and provide health insurance for my kids. Once my husband left, I cried because I wasn't sure how I was going to manage. But it didn't take long before I realized I was already doing everything anyway. The only things I hadn't been doing were mowing the lawn and taking out the trash.

While working in the grocery store, I recognized I was becoming cynical because every time I would see a couple walking together holding hands, I would think, "Enjoy it while it lasts, because it won't." It was during this time that I felt as though no one would be interested in a twice divorced mother of three. Following my divorce from my second husband, I enjoyed the single life every Friday night. For the first time, I would go out to bars with friends. At first, it was fun but I soon realized that every week I would see the same lonely people. This was not a lifestyle I wanted to continue. Initially, I thought having three kids would prevent anyone from pursuing me. It didn't take long for me to realize that because of my kids, I was able to weed out men who wouldn't be right for me. My children were a blessing that enabled only special people to enter my life. My friends had to kiss a lot of toads before they found someone worth spending time with. My children spared me from all that. If I told someone about my kids and they disappeared, then they weren't right for me anyway. While praying to God, I would pray that if he was going to send another man to be a part of my life that he would be good to my kids. That was the most important quality that I was looking for.

The job that provided our health insurance was my position in the grocery store. One day, I was working in the express lane and had my head down scanning groceries when I heard a loud bang from someone slamming a six pack of beer on my counter. I looked up and saw Joe. I couldn't believe it. He looked terrible. His hair was long and had hair color in it from him attending cosmetology school. He never got his license, but he did learn some haircutting skills that have come in handy over the years. He was also heavier than I had ever seen him. The circumstances of his life and the effect they were having on him were obvious from his appearance.

It happened to be time for my break, so I was able to step away from my check stand. We chatted briefly and made plans to go to dinner and catch up.

Joe was so broke that he needed to get a "comp" from his dad, who was the catering director at one of the local hotels. He was divorced, living with his parents and had full custody of his severely handicapped six-year-old son. I was aware of his son since our mothers worked together at one of the larger retail stores at the mall.

Joe's son had been born perfectly healthy, weighing almost 10 pounds. He was eight weeks old when Joe's wife returned to work. Their next-door neighbor ran a day care out of her home and she was caring for Justin. Two days after Justin received his first set of baby vaccines, he was napping when the provider's 2-year-old came into the room. The toddler liked to pull the blankets off the babies when they slept. When his mom hurried into the room after him, she found Justin was not breathing, and his lips were turning blue. The provider immediately grabbed him and started CPR while calling 911. By the time Joe and his wife arrived at the hospital, Justin was hooked up to all kinds of monitors with tubes and wires all over his small body. Joe barely recognized his son. He had monitors measuring the pressure on his brain, his blood pressure and more. A CT scan showed brain damage. A few days later, the nurses disconnected the monitors to send Justin for another CT scan. When he returned to his room, the monitors were reconnected. Joe noticed that the monitor measuring the pressure on Justin's brain was no longer increasing as it had been, and he mentioned it to Justin's nurse. She told Joe that it meant that Justin was probably coming out of the induced coma. Eventually, the level on one of the monitors reached zero, which meant Justin should have been dead. Joe

instinctively knew there was something wrong and started yelling at
the nurse to get a doctor. After inspecting the equipment, it was
discovered that the leads on the monitors had been crossed and
incorrectly hooked up.

After the errors had been corrected, Joe and his wife were led
into a nearby room and asked what they had heard. They were vague
with their answers. They both knew they needed an attorney.

Justin's brain damage was so severe that the only brain activity
was around his brain stem. He only had survival instincts. He could
swallow and cry when he was in pain or uncomfortable, but his brain
would never recover from the injury. Justin remained the equivalent
of an eight-week-old infant until he died. The doctors ruled it as an
aborted crib death. Justin would have died if the provider hadn't
walked in and interrupted the crib death in progress. Unfortunately,
no one ever made the connection with Justin's episode and the baby
vaccines that he had just had days before. Today, it would be ruled a
vaccine injury based on the time between the vaccination and the
actual incident.

Joe filled me in on all of this during our dinner. He explained
that he lived with his parents, so they could help care for Justin
while he was working. Joe's mother worked during the day and
when she got home at night, Joe would leave for work as a food
server.

This was not the first time our paths had crossed since we first
worked together at the grocery store. Like I mentioned, our mothers
worked together at the same store for 17 years. One day I was at the
mall in that store with my grandmother. I looked up from the rack,
and there he was. The beautiful man with black curly hair, green
eyes and million-dollar smile was standing there looking at me. My
heart skipped a beat. We barely had a chance to say hello before his
mother appeared. He was there to pick her up from work.

Another time, I was driving down the street when I heard a horn
honking. I looked to my left and there he was again. He was driving
alongside me and motioning for me to pull over. When he got out of
his car, he was wearing a cast on his leg. He was recovering from
knee surgery. The injuries from being an all-star soccer player had

taken their toll. We were able to chat for a few moments before going on our way.

I have often thought that God kept putting us in one another's path so we wouldn't forget about each other.

On my first trip to Disneyland with my girls, we ran into Joe again. I was with my soon-to-be second husband, and Joe was with his soon-to-be wife. We were standing in line at one of the many snack shacks inside the park. As we introduced our significant others, I found myself thinking, "I didn't think I was pretty enough for Joe to ask me out, and he is marrying her?" I know it wasn't very nice, but it was the truth (at least in my eyes at the time). I began to think there may be hope after all. Looking back, I should have realized that those thoughts alone were a red flag. I shouldn't have been considering marrying another man when I had these strong feelings for Joe.

We would run into each other yet again at the grocery store. Joe and his wife had just brought their newborn daughter home from the hospital. I congratulated them both and went on my way.

I saw him another time, but this time he didn't see me. It was my 30th birthday and a guy friend decided I shouldn't be alone. We met at a cozy bar on the strip for a drink when he got off work. We were sitting in a booth when I looked up and saw Joe across from us, cuddling with another woman. I told my date that we needed to leave. He was confused, so I explained that I knew the guy in the booth across from us and the woman was not his wife. It may not have made sense to my date, but I wanted to avoid the uncomfortable exchange that would have followed once Joe noticed I was sitting directly across from him and his mistress.

Not surprisingly, Joe was divorced shortly after this sighting.

When we finally went to dinner, I considered it old friends getting together to catch up. We had a great time, but I still wasn't prepared when he called me the following day to say that he was interested in dating. I couldn't believe this beautiful man was finally asking me out after 13 years. Now I worried that if we started dating and it didn't work out, we would no longer be friends. I didn't want to risk losing his friendship. Joe was persistent and ultimately persuaded me to take the risk. Eventually we introduced our kids to one another. We spent more and more time together and things were going well.

One day Joe and I went to the mall to pick up some pictures he had taken of his two kids. We were waiting in a small room when a young girl came in with the pictures. She opened the envelope and pulled them out. As she started laying them on the table, she began to laugh at the pictures. It is obvious that Justin is severely handicapped by looking at the pictures. Joe and I were shocked at her behavior and were speechless. I was very new to being around Justin, but I still knew how offended Joe was that this girl was laughing at his son. He took the minimum number of pictures offered and we couldn't get out of there quick enough. If that had happened after we were married, I would have reacted quite differently. I would have insisted on speaking to a manager and reporting the incident. There really was no excuse for anyone to laugh at someone's disabled child.

After about five months, Joe asked me to marry him. I was not prepared for it and wouldn't give him an answer. After two failed marriages, I needed more time. The thought of blending our two families terrified me. I wasn't sure what our future looked like with five kids—one with disabilities—and multiple parents. You must admit that on paper, this looked like a recipe for disaster.

One night we decided to take all the kids to a drive-in movie. I had a minivan, so Justin was able to lie comfortably on one of the bench seats, while the other children camped out on the roof of the van. We no sooner got all the kids settled in when it started. One after another, we heard requests for something to eat or a trip to the bathroom. Each request was followed by a child climbing down through the open window. This continued throughout the movie. I was waiting for Joe to lose his cool and pack everything up to go home. After all, it didn't seem as though any of the kids were watching the movie. To my surprise, Joe appeared to be having a good time. It was at that moment that I looked at him and said, "Okay, if this is your idea of a good time, then I will marry you because this is my life." He couldn't believe I had just accepted his proposal. Although he doesn't like me to mention it, he began to cry.

When we told our parents that we were getting married, the responses were unexpected. Joe's parents told him the only reason I wanted to marry him was because I needed help raising my three kids. My parents told me the only reason Joe wanted to marry me was because he needed help with his severely handicapped son. I'd like to think both sets of parents had our best interests in their hearts. What they didn't realize is that they were telling us we were 'unlovable' because of our kids. In fact, Joe's mother had previously told him that he'd better get used to being alone because no one would ever love him because of Justin.

Just to be clear, I was very concerned about adding a severely handicapped little boy to my family. I didn't know what I was capable of as far as Justin's care was concerned. I wondered how I would handle diaper changes as he grew into a young adult. I ultimately decided that I wouldn't make my decision to marry Joe based on Justin. I figured I would let God handle that. I based my decision solely on my feelings for him.

We were married on January 1, 1990. The day before the wedding, Justin was admitted to the hospital with bronchitis. We had to decide whether to go ahead with the ceremony or postpone it. We went ahead with our plans and then headed to the hospital in our wedding attire.

Our wedding picture. I love that my three year old, red headed nephew insisted on being in the picture with us.

Although Justin had been hospitalized every year with either bronchitis or pneumonia, this would be the last time during our marriage that he would be hospitalized with either illness. Justin thrived while living with our other kids. In fact, we used to tell people that Justin was our perfect child. He never talked back. He didn't mess up the house. He was truly an angel and was without sin. We learned that some of us were sent here to learn and others to teach. Justin taught us so many things. All our children witnessed the unconditional love Joe had for his son. Justin taught our kids about compassion. Our oldest son, Nick, became a paramedic/fire-fighter and was totally comfortable running calls on patients in Justin's condition. Nick was feeding Justin through his feeding tube when he was about 12 years old. He never hesitated to help Joe once Justin's feeding tube was put in place.

One night, Joe and I had a rare date night. We ended up drinking tequila with unexpected results. I wasn't a very big drinker and hadn't had tequila before. It seems that tequila causes me to be quite combative. Joe, on the other hand, becomes disgustingly mushy and "lovey dovey." He kept saying, "I luuuuv you."

When we went out to my minivan to drive home, we had a flat

tire. We began arguing, and I decided I would just walk home. Let me begin by saying we were not in an area where I had any business walking alone late at night. Joe didn't know what to do. While he was in the middle of changing the tire, I took off walking. It was late and I was headed to my parents' house. To get to their house, I needed to walk through even rougher areas. Joe hurried to get the tire changed. Before I got there, Joe finished changing the tire and tried to find me. I had gone one direction, and Joe went another. He arrived at my parents' house first and woke them up. When they came to the door, he asked them if they knew where I was. This was not a good scene. Before I got there, Joe also called our house and woke up my daughter asking if I was there. She became upset and wanted to know what he had done with her mother. Now there were two houses awake and upset. After we left my parents' house, we continued to argue. I had purchased a new set of golf clubs for Joe with a bonus I received from work. I had never gotten a bonus before, but I didn't hesitate to spend it all on him. He had never owned a new set of golf clubs, and I thought he deserved them. While we were arguing, I found the need to throw it in his face that I had been so generous. As soon as I did this, Joe pulled the minivan over. We happened to be at a wash where the water ran after a heavy rain. Joe got out of the van, opened the back, grabbed his golf clubs and threw them over the guard rail into the wash area. I was shocked. Joe got back in the van, and we drove home in complete silence. We went to bed and sobered up. We made up in the morning and decided we should go back to find the golf clubs. When we arrived at the location, Joe had me stand watch while he climbed over the guard rail and went into the wash. We both knew homeless people hung out in the area and we were a little scared. When Joe got in the wash, he saw his golf clubs lying neatly in a row. It was obvious that a homeless person had discovered them and was looking to turn them into some cash. Joe quickly gathered up his clubs and yelled for me to get in the car. We took off safely and intact. This is one of the stories that proves it was a good thing alcohol has not been involved in the past 30 years of our marriage.

As if having five children between us wasn't enough, we decided to have another one. You would think it would happen effortlessly since we both had children. For some reason, I could not get pregnant. During our first year of marriage, I went to the doctor twice to see if there was something preventing me from getting pregnant. The doctor assured me that everything was fine.

Shortly after our first anniversary, we began having problems. In fact, we had such a bad fight that Joe took Justin and went back to his parents' house. That night I took a pregnancy test and, of course, it came back positive. Joe returned the next day to get his belongings. While he was there, I showed him the positive pregnancy test. His response was "I guess that's your problem."

Here I was pregnant and a mother of three. How was I going to manage? My concern was that this new baby would be a burden and responsibility for the children I already had. In my mind, this was not fair, and while I never would have thought it possible, I considered an abortion. It was an option, but I knew I couldn't go through with it. God and I had a conversation. I told him he had a strange sense of humor. I had no idea what his plan was, but I was going to trust him. Surrendering to him was my only option. Trying to figure out my future was just too overwhelming.

As you can imagine, I was not at all happy with Joe. We didn't speak for about three weeks. One night while I was at work at the grocery store, I was walking back from my break, when I saw Joe standing near the entrance to the store. He wanted to talk, so I asked the manager for a few more minutes. As I stood in front of him with my arms crossed, my body language made it clear that I really wasn't interested in anything he had to say. Regardless, he began to tell me that a few years prior, he had a problem with drugs. He explained that he thought he had it under control, but he didn't. Hearing this, I was shocked and couldn't believe what he was saying. Expecting him to tell me he was smoking pot, I was in disbelief when he told me he was using cocaine. When I asked him how long he had been using, he said seven months.

As I stood there listening to Joe, I began to get extremely angry. He was living in my house with my kids and using cocaine. He agreed to get help. I insisted he go to an inpatient facility to get treatment. It was so hard not to hug him and tell him everything was going to be all right. Instead, I turned and walked away with tears running down my face. Joe had to know he could not be a part of my life if he was using cocaine.

Joe drove himself to a treatment center and checked in to a 90-day program for drug and alcohol abuse. I was so naive that I didn't even realize he was an alcoholic. The kids and I were also involved in his program; we all needed to recover.

Prior to Joe revealing his cocaine addiction, I had been an avid coupon clipper to save money on our grocery bill. Once I understood that while I was spending hours every week creating menus and clipping coupons, Joe was taking the money I saved and putting it up his nose, I refused to EVER clip a coupon again. I won't clip coupons to this day.

To make ends meet, we had to become a little creative. We used checks to pay for things when we were first married. I was paid weekly but Joe was paid biweekly. On the weeks he didn't receive a paycheck, we would usually run out of money. I would pay the bills, put gas in our vehicles and buy groceries. Unfortunately, I was aware when I wrote the check for groceries that I probably didn't have enough money in the bank to cover the check. The check usually took two days to clear the bank. The day after I wrote a check that I knew wouldn't clear, I would need to write another check for cash to cover the check that was going to be short. We had two bank accounts, so one day we would write a check from one account, and deposit it in the other account. We would repeat this every day until payday came and then we would start all over again. This was our way of robbing Peter to pay Paul. We were actually borrowing money from ourselves.

One day Joe was in a local Walmart, and he wrote a check. The cashier took his check, ran it through a little machine and then handed the check back to him. He was confused and asked her what she had done. She explained they had just taken the money out of our account. You should have seen the look on his face. It became clear that we would no longer be able to continue our little check-cashing system. Not long after that, debit cards were issued from banks and checks no longer took two days to clear the bank. Fortunately, by the time this was happening, our income was increasing, and we no longer needed to float checks. I'm not sure how we would have made it during those years if debit cards had been in use.

My son was very excited when Joe and I got married. The day before our wedding, he told his sisters that he couldn't wait to call Joe "Dad." When Joe moved out, he lost that title. My son never called him Dad again. I think he felt betrayed and abandoned. It would take a lot of time to rebuild that trust between them. My son now calls Joe "Pops."

It became clear that the help Joe received from his parents with Justin came at a very high cost. Because they had helped him, he now owed them. Whenever Joe's parents' lawn needed to be mowed, his mother would call Joe and tell him. It was expected that he would drop everything and go mow their lawn. Most days Joe was exhausted from working graveyard shifts. Daily, he would get up from broken sleep to get Justin ready for the bus to pick him up and transport him to school. We also had a new baby and were raising six kids together. They were never concerned that Joe's plate was full. I constantly worried about him and his newfound sobriety. It still amazes me how he survived it all.

CHAPTER 5

*A*nyone who has dealt with an addict knows that rehab is just the beginning of a long road. Joe moved back in following his treatment, but trust continued to be an issue.

A few months following the completion of Joe's treatment, our son was born. The baby was probably the reason Joe decided to get treatment. Once he knew I was pregnant, he understood I would never allow him to be a part of any of the kids' lives if he was involved with drugs. It appears God did have a plan after all. God knew when the time would be right for me to finally get pregnant. I like to think that our son saved Joe's life.

It was a week before my due date and I went to my doctor's appointment. While the doctor was examining me, he accidentally broke my water. He told me to go home and wake up my hubby and he would meet us at the hospital. By the time we arrived at the hospital, my contractions had started. Joe had never witnessed a live birth since his other kids had been born via C-section. Joe stood with the doctor and watched our son's head crown. The baby had a ton of dark hair and Joe would later tell me he thought I was taking a crap.

The baby was born without any complications. He was beautiful and weighed 8 lbs. He was my smallest baby as far as his weight but had a big head. When the nurse was measuring the baby's head, she said, "What a melon head!" I was lying in my bed thinking, "Hey lady, I just pushed that out of my body… give me a break!"

When the pediatrician came in to check on our son, we told him we wanted to put the baby on an apnea monitor since they considered Justin's episode to be an aborted crib death. Prior to our son's birth, we had researched crib deaths. Statistically, our baby fell into every risk category there was. He was a boy. He would be less than four months old during the winter months including flu season. He had a sibling that suffered from an aborted crib death. We explained all this to the doctor and his response was, "Do you know how much my health insurance premiums were last month?" This was not what we expected. Joe lost his mind and started yelling at the doctor. The doctor left our room and Joe chased him down the hallway yelling; "I have one retarded son, I'm not going to have another one!" Everyone on the floor could hear the yelling. A nurse came in and told us she heard what had happened. She informed us that there was a new doctor practicing at the hospital, and she could contact him for us. We agreed since there was no way we would ever let the other pediatrician near our baby. In less than 20 minutes, the new doctor arrived. We explained our situation and again requested our son be put on an apnea monitor. The new doctor told us that if it would help us sleep at night, he would be happy to set us up with the monitor. We were so grateful and relieved. We loved our son's pediatrician and he continued to see him until he was almost 18 years old.

Family photo at baby's baptism

EVEN THOUGH WE loved one another, we still struggled in our marriage. Eventually we would separate again. As much as I wanted our marriage to work, it wasn't happening. While continuing to work with the marriage and family counselor that Joe and I had been seeing, I tried to figure out why my third marriage was failing. Why did I keep choosing men who were not right for me? As this was occurring, I tried to encourage Joe to also continue counseling on his own, but he refused. He felt our sessions were nothing more than an opportunity to "tattletale."

During our separation, my high school friend and former boyfriend visited again. We went to dinner and caught up with each other's lives. We both had been struggling with our marriages and we shared the ways we were navigating through those challenges. He asked me if anyone had suggested a book that had helped him. When he told me the title, I told him that, as a matter of fact, two other people had suggested I read the same book. One of those people was our marriage counselor. I wasn't interested in self-help books at the time, so I had ignored the suggestion. Now there was a third person recommending it to me.

After my friend left town, I had another conversation with God. I told him I was getting the message, and I went out and purchased the book. The book's author is John Bradshaw, and the book is called "On the Family." He has written several books, but this was the one that saved our lives.

The book was fascinating. It spoke of birth order and its effects on how we react to things. As I read, I envision myself and my siblings and found that the information lined up. I then applied what I had read to my children and to my mother and her siblings. The more I read, the more intrigued I was. The book also addressed the way children of alcoholics and victims of sexual abuse react to certain situations. As I read each scenario, I kept saying to myself "Joe does that." I was a little confused, because Joe and I had never discussed anything regarding sexual abuse.

During this time, Joe came to pick up our son for a visit. The baby was sleeping, so I asked him if he wanted to come in and wait for him to wake up. We sat at the kitchen table and talked. We hadn't spoken for several weeks. I began to tell him about the book and the three different recommendations. I described the things I found fascinating. Finally, I told him that he had a lot of behaviors that the book described for victims of sexual abuse. He didn't react, so I just figured I was reading way too much into it. The baby woke up and Joe took him to his parent's house where he was still staying.

A few hours passed before I received a call from Joe asking me if I had the phone number for our family therapist. I was a bit annoyed because I knew he could find her number in the phone book (yes, we still used them then). After all, I had been suggesting he go to counseling on his own for over two months. After a pause, I reluctantly gave him the number. After another pause, he admitted that my guess about sexual abuse was correct.

I was unaware that during his stay in the rehab facility, there was a day when his parents attended a group session, and the topic was sexual abuse. Joe described his parents as being extremely uncomfortable during the conversation. As Joe sat there, he thought to himself, "Of all days for his parents to be here." His parents' presence prevented him from speaking openly about his abuse.

My heart stopped; I was shocked. Eventually he shared that he had been abused by both his brothers and his mother. We knew he needed to get out of that house.

Joe began therapy again. As he started to navigate through his recovery, he investigated moving to an apartment. Ultimately, he decided to move back in with me.

I initially struggled with Joe and his therapy. I was young and still very insecure. I didn't understand why he couldn't talk to me the way he talked with our therapist. I wasn't jealous of her, but I was jealous that he trusted her with things he was not able to tell me. I eventually got over myself and became thankful that he trusted her enough to get the help he needed.

The revelation of sexual abuse explained Joe's alcohol and drug addiction. He was unconsciously using them to numb his pain.

During this time, his father's health took a turn for the worse. He was suffering from congestive heart failure. Because of his dad's poor health, Joe was not comfortable talking to him about the abuse. Joe's dad was dependent on care from his mother. If Joe told him about the abuse, his father would need to make a decision. Deep down, I think Joe feared that he might side with his wife out of necessity. Besides, the news itself could kill him.

Joe's aunt (his dad's sister) and uncle were among the visitors at the hospital. Joe used the opportunity to take them aside and tell them what his mother had done. Joe was crushed when they ignored what he had told them. He felt they either didn't believe him, or they chose to side with his mother. He felt alone and betrayed.

This was an extremely tough time. It was all I could do to hide my emotions when I was around Joe's mother, but I couldn't risk jeopardizing Joe's time with his dying father. All I knew was Joe's mother belonged in jail.

I would find out the extent of Joe's abuse as he navigated his way through his recovery. At the same time, Joe knew that he was losing his father—the one person in his immediate family who never abused him.

As a family, we were dealing with a lot. Our kids were still young enough that we couldn't really share the adult version of what had happened to Joe. They had already been through Joe's rehab which hopefully was a learning experience. I'd like to think that as difficult as it was, my kids never made bad decisions regarding drugs or alcohol because of what we had experienced as a family. Joe and I had to be vigilant when the kids were around his mother during this difficult time. She was no longer a grandmother figure; she was now a predator. I felt like I was in charge of protecting everyone. I was determined not to let Joe's mother hurt him anymore and even more determined to keep my children safe.

CHAPTER 6

The first story of abuse that Joe was brave enough to share with me involved his oldest brother. He looked up to his big brother, so when he was asked to get in bed with him, he complied. His brother persuaded him to touch and masturbate him. Joe was young enough that he didn't know any better, but his brother did.

Joe's other brother also abused him. Joe remembered coming home from middle school and falling asleep on the floor. He was face down, lying on his stomach, when he was awakened by his brother on top of him. His brother had pulled Joe's pants down and was attempting to penetrate him. Joe immediately began fighting his brother to get off him. His brother tried to convince him that it would feel good, but Joe was able to successfully wrestle his brother off.

These two incidents make me wonder what happened to his brothers for them to do such things to him. Were they victims too? It is common for victims who do not get professional help to become predators.

During one of my sessions with our family therapist, she shared that through her practice, she had heard all kinds of stories of abuse, but she had never cried until she heard Joe describe the regular abuse he received from his mother.

Joe told her that as a little boy, he was required to call his mother into the bathroom before he finished taking his shower. She needed to make sure he was clean. His mother always grabbed the soap and lathered her hands to wash and masturbate her little boy. She would also insert her finger to check for cleanliness. To Joe, this was normal behavior. He figured all mothers did this to their children. It wasn't until he was older that this ritual became more and more uncomfortable. When he was about 10 years old, he recalls having to call his mother into the shower. He was full of anxiety as he rubbed a bar of soap between his fingers and his thumb. He knew if he didn't call her in, he would get in trouble. Anxiety growing, he rubbed and rubbed until the soap had a hole in the middle of it. That was the story that drove our therapist to tears. Picturing a young boy standing in the shower filled with fear, rubbing and rubbing that bar of soap and not wanting to call for his mother was more than she could handle.

The worst story Joe shared with me happened when he was 5 or 6 years old. His family lived in Michigan at the time. Joe's two older brothers were going to pick wild blueberries. Joe wanted to go with them, but his mother wouldn't let him. He was so upset that he crawled into bed and cried himself to sleep. He awakened to severe pain. He was face down and on his knees with his wrists tied to his ankles. He struggled and, while reaching back, he could feel leather straps and buckles. Because of his age, Joe couldn't understand what was happening and had no idea his mother had strapped on an artificial penis and was raping him. When his mother was finished, he heard her laughing as she walked out of the room. He never told anyone what happened, because he was afraid of what his mother would do to him while his dad was working.

These stories of abuse explained why Joe stuttered when we first were married. His stuttering has gone away since his treatment and recovery. It's not uncommon for children who have experienced trauma to stutter.

Whenever Joe's dad would ask him to go fishing or hunting, he would always go—not because he liked to hunt or fish, but because he knew no one would hurt him if he was with his father. Joe's memories of hunting with his dad were miserable. He remembers the rain and the cold, but regardless of how uncomfortable he was, he was safe. If he stayed home, there would be opportunity for his mother or brothers to abuse him.

CHAPTER 7

$\mathcal{W}$e continued to work on our marriage as Joe maintained his sobriety. I'm not sure where he found the strength. He had given up drugs and alcohol and was coming to terms with his childhood abuse. His father was dying from congestive heart failure, and Joe was unable to talk to him about any of it. He feared that telling his father about the abuse would kill him. If that happened, the rest of the family would blame him for his father's death.

Joe also lived with the fear of finding out that his dad knew about the abuse. How would he handle it if his father knew all along and didn't protect him?

I really wanted Joe to tell his dad while he still could, but it wasn't for me to decide. Joe would have to live with the results of telling him, but also with the ramifications of never sharing something so life changing with his dad.

One evening, Joe's dad sent everyone home from the hospital. Joe stopped in to see his dad before he headed to his graveyard shift at work. He said goodnight to his father not knowing it would be the last time he would see him alive. Following the death of his father,

Joe tried to maintain some sort of relationship with his family. It was a promise he had made to his dad. After several weeks, it became clear that he would not be able to keep that promise. Joe told his mother to stay out of his life, and she did. There was no attempt to reach out to him for almost 30 years.

After Joe's mother died in 2020, he thought his brothers might try to reach out to him, but that didn't happen. In fact, when her obituary was written, there was no mention that Joe even existed. I guess the brothers were attempting to "cancel" him.

When I was pregnant with our son, I was very curious to see what Joe looked like as a baby. We searched through his family's early pictures but couldn't find any baby pictures of him. One day when his grandmother (mother's mom) was visiting, she mentioned something about his strawberry birthmark that covered his entire left cheek. She told me that when he turned 5, it suddenly disappeared. It all began to make sense. Joe had a large birthmark on his face that must have embarrassed his mother. That is why there are no baby pictures of him. Once the birthmark went away, there are pictures of Joe as a little boy.

When Joe and his brothers were growing up, his parents refused to teach them Spanish. They didn't want their sons to speak with an accent. Because of this, Joe never had a conversation with his paternal grandparents, who didn't speak English. When Joe's family visited them in New Mexico, his cousins had to translate for him and his brothers whenever his grandparents wanted to talk to them. Joe's parents even changed the spelling of their name so it would appear Italian instead of Mexican. I'm not going to judge. I know my own cousins denied being French. For some reason, their parents told them they were not French. We would laugh at them and tell them our moms were sisters and we were part French from my mom's side, so they had to be French too. Those same cousins did their ancestry DNA, and we can see their results since they come up as a match. My cousins have twice as much French DNA as we do. Both of their parents are part French. I wish I could have seen their faces when they received their results. I'm not going to lie—the thought of it made me chuckle.

Joe discovered that his last name is the name of a family who took in his great-grandfather after his great-grandfather's mother died. Following the death of his mother, his great-grandfather's father remarried. Apparently, the new stepmother wasn't very nice to Joe's great-grandfather, so he ran away. Another family took him in, and he took their family name. Unfortunately, we don't know the correct spelling of the original family name. Maybe one day we will have the time to research his family history to figure all this out.

I have never been so glad that I maintained my maiden name when Joe and I married. If I had taken Joe's last name, I would have been upset finding out it really wasn't his family's name. There were several reasons I kept my maiden name. I had already changed my name twice with previous marriages. It is such a pain to change all the legal documents once you marry. I didn't want to deal with it again. Also, there were two other women in our town walking around with Joe's last name. One was his mother, and the other was his ex. I did not ever want to be confused with either one of them. The last reason was that despite the fact my parents had five kids, there were only two boys and one of them never had kids. The brother with kids had a boy and girl. There was only one boy in our family who could carry on our family name. If he didn't have a boy, the name would end. Fortunately, my nephew had his baby boy and our family's name sake. My grandfather was the first, my father the second, my brother the third, my nephew the fourth and now his son, the fifth.

Joe and I also gave our son both of our last names, and we figured he could choose which one he wanted to use. As an adult, he uses both our names with a hyphen.

Joe and I worked hard to reestablish trust between us. One day I felt the need to check his car to make sure he wasn't using. Joe had revealed that his car was where he hid his drugs. He was taking a shower when I snuck out to his car to look. While I was searching his car, I let one fly. Yes, I farted. Today, I guess they would say I "hot boxed" Joe. I came back into the house believing I was in the clear. Joe kissed me goodbye and went out to his car to go to work. Within minutes, he was back, and he was livid. He told me he knew I had searched his car. I asked him how he knew (dumb question), and he told me he could smell the gift I had left behind. He was upset that I didn't trust him, because he hadn't done anything to warrant the search of his car. He was still seeing a counselor from the rehab facility he had attended and felt the need to share the story. The counselor did remind Joe that it was his actions that had caused the mistrust between us.

A few years passed as we attempted to repair our relationship while raising our kids. Our son was starting kindergarten. We had been married for eight years and hadn't had the money or resources to take a real family vacation. We finally had the opportunity to use a time share we had purchased years earlier. If we were going to travel, we needed to find a nursing home or rehabilitation center for Joe's son, since Justin's mother refused to care for him while we were away. We also needed to get court approval to pay for the care. Once the judge approved the expense, we could make our vacation arrangements.

Joe's daughter was living with her mother during this time. A week before we were to leave on our vacation, Joe's ex suddenly dropped his daughter off on our doorstep forcing us to change our existing travel plans to include her. We had to pay extra to change our travel arrangements in addition to the added expenses of bringing another person along. We were already strapped for money, and the new expenses cut into our spending money for the trip.

Once we returned home, Joe's daughter wanted to go back and live with her mother. Although we weren't surprised, that meant more money that we didn't have would be needed for an attorney. This was just one of many times his daughter would change her living arrangements. Thousands of dollars were spent on attorney's fees in family court. Joe and I both agree that the seven years we spent in family court were the most difficult and stressful years of our entire marriage.

Our final family court hearing lasted four hours. While Joe was on the stand answering questions, he looked over to the monitor on the Judge's elevated desk. He couldn't believe it when he noticed she was playing solitaire on her computer. If the Judge hadn't been so unstable, I'm sure he would have said something. He was furious. This person was about to make decisions regarding our lives, and here she was playing solitaire instead of paying attention to the testimony. Fortunately, that was the last time we would go before her. Shortly thereafter, she was removed from the bench and entered a mental health facility. Her abrasive treatment and verbiage had been extremely inappropriate, and I walked out of her courtroom on more than one occasion. Unfortunately, Joe had to sit there and take the abuse.

A few months after our vacation, school began. One morning, we woke as usual and ventured out of our bedroom to start getting the kids ready. Joe headed towards our family room where Justin slept on his daybed, while I continued down the hallway towards the kids' bedrooms. As I was waking the kids, I heard a bloodcurdling scream from Joe. By the sound of his voice, I knew it was Justin. I ran to the family room and found Joe collapsed and sobbing on the floor next to Justin's bed.

Justin had died in his sleep. I grabbed the phone and called 911. The dispatcher wanted to know if we wanted to try CPR. I'm sure she was confused when I said no. If you have seen someone who has died, you know. I explained Justin's condition to her, and she began to understand.

Within minutes we had police and paramedics in our home. They pronounced Justin deceased and notified the coroner. While we were waiting for the coroner, we let the other kids say goodbye to Justin. Once Joe was able to compose himself, he called his ex to let her know Justin was gone.

One of the police officers who responded was a regular customer at the grocery store where I worked. I didn't really know him, but after Justin's death, he would frequently come into the store and, if I was working, he would come through my line. He was constantly checking on us—wanting to be sure we were okay. His kindness touched our hearts, and he remains a special friend to this day.

While I was working at the police department, we had an officer shot. I distinctly remember the radio traffic during those tense moments. The officer who was shot was a friend of mine, which heightened the situation. The officer had tried to kick in a door where a suspect was holed up. They were ready and in position. What they weren't prepared for was the officer's foot going through the hollow door. As he struggled to pull his leg back, the suspect shot him in the leg. They were able to quickly pull him back and I heard his sergeant say, "Hang in there, buddy, we're going to get you out of here." I recognized his sergeant's voice as the same officer who offered us his kindness. He was keeping his officer calm and safe until the paramedics got him the medical attention he needed. I'm happy to say that the officer recovered from his injuries and was able to return to work. I gained more admiration and respect for the sergeant that day.

I read the eulogy at Justin's funeral. Part of it included a letter from Justin to Joe. I told him that I had a dream, and Justin spoke to me. He asked me to read this letter to his dad:

Dear Daddy,

I know I never got to call your name out so you could understand it, but I am saying it now. Daddy, I know we never got to play catch or go fishing, but I am free to do it now. I know I drooled and spit up on you, and you never got mad. I threw up on you many times, and you never got mad. I soiled my diapers terribly, and you never got mad. On the occasions my stomach would ache, you would hold me as I cried even though you were exhausted, and you never got mad. My endless doctors' appointments took up so many of your days off, and you never got mad. You stayed home so many times when you wanted to be somewhere else, and you never got mad. It became more and more difficult for you to lift, dress and bathe me as I grew and became heavier, and you never got mad. I will miss our weekly jacuzzi baths as you would sit and hold me while you exercised my stiff body. You knew how much I enjoyed these baths. I would feel so good when we were through. As you massaged lotion into my dry skin, I savored your touch, but most of all I enjoyed my time alone with you. All you ever did was love me. For that, I will always love you

*too. Thank you, Daddy, for the years of love, sacrifice and devotion
you have given me. I love you and will be in your heart forever.*

    Love, Justin

    P.S. Daddy, I'm okay...

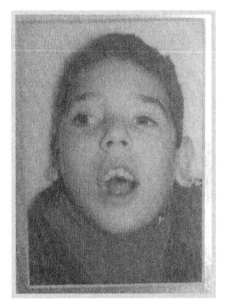

Justin RIP

We managed to get through Justin's funeral, but we remained
emotionally fragile. We would reach a moment of normalcy, and then
we would run into a friend or neighbor who would express their
condolences. These interactions would start another round of tears
and grief. We finally made the decision to take the two youngest kids
out of town with us to get away from the "well-wishers." We understand that these people were just trying to say or do the right thing,
but it was just too much for us and we needed a break. We later
learned we were accused of taking the kids out of town to celebrate.
This was very hurtful and the furthest thing from the truth. I had a
friend tell me that it was a blessing that Justin died because he was
no longer suffering. I asked that friend to please never say that in

front of Joe. We never believed Justin was suffering. As long as he was fed and his diaper was dry, he was a happy little boy. Hearing people say that he was now in a "better place" was also painful to hear. I know Joe thought, "How could it be a better place when Justin wasn't with him?" We understand that it is hard to know what to say to someone who is grieving. Unless you have buried a child, you will never understand that unique grief. That includes a child with disabilities or one who has been through a long illness. Don't try to minimize it or comfort the parents by trying to tell them it's a blessing that their child is gone.

We didn't realize it at the time, but when a child dies at home, regardless of the circumstances, an investigation is conducted. A complete autopsy was performed on Justin. We were standing in line at the bank when Joe finally received a call from the coroner. Joe stepped out of line and sat in a nearby chair to take the phone call. The coroner began the conversation by asking Joe what had happened to Justin. He told her about his aborted crib death that was the cause of his brain damage. She told Joe she had never seen someone with Justin's deficits in such good condition and so well cared for. Justin never suffered from a diaper rash or bed sores. It really was quite remarkable, and Joe deserves all the credit.

The coroner assured Joe that Justin did not suffer. She explained that it was as if God reached down and flipped a switch and turned off his brain. She told Joe that it could not have been prevented or predicted and once it started, it could not be stopped. This was exactly what Joe needed to hear.

Joe had gotten up in the middle of the night—just a few hours before he found Justin dead. He sat in his recliner next to Justin's bed while he ate an ice cream sandwich and listened to Justin snore. Joe had been questioning himself and wondering if he had missed something. The explanation from the coroner eased his mind.

There are so many things that you learn from having a severely handicapped child. I didn't even realize Justin would be attending school. After all, he wasn't going to be able to learn to read and write. We would attend his parent/teacher conferences and discuss things like his ability to swallow. Justin's school day consisted of lots of physical therapy-type activities. His teachers were amazing, and I recognized what special people they were. It was during one of those parent/teacher conferences we attended that we discovered our youngest son needed speech therapy. We were with the principal of Justin's school, and we had brought our 3-year-old son with us. While the adults were speaking, our toddler was trying to tell us something. As we tried to decipher what he was saying, the principle asked us if we had ever had him evaluated. We were totally confused. In my mind, I was thinking, "Wait, we are here for Justin." Our son didn't speak very clearly, but he was able to communicate. It was our complete "parent fail" to not notice how behind he was with his speech. We followed up with an evaluation and were advised to have him join the school's speech therapy program soon after.

The speech therapy took place at the school our son would be attending. This was a blessing because whenever we asked our son if he wanted to go to school, he would tell us, "No." Our little boy told us he wasn't going to go to school until he was big like Nick, his big brother. His brother was 14 years old so that wasn't going to work. By attending speech therapy, he was exposed to the school and the thought of going to school wasn't so overwhelming for him. In fact, while he attended speech therapy the teachers running the head start program asked if our son could come into their room following his speech therapy. They wanted to use him as a "model" child as an example of good behavior for the other children. We were very happy with their request because our son had never attended pre-school and although he had many siblings, it would be beneficial for him to be socialized with other kids his age before starting school.

A couple of years before he died, Justin developed a hump on his back that we needed to have looked at. Scoliosis is common in chil-dren in Justin's condition. We took him to a pediatric orthopedic surgeon who ruled out Scoliosis but informed us that Justin would most likely need surgery in the future. Because Justin never walked, his hip sockets didn't formed. When this occurs, it causes the legs to cross making diaper changes and personal hygiene almost impossible. The surgeon explained that he would need to surgically cut the groin muscles to enable the hygiene care. This news was extremely upsetting. When we arrived home, I sat on the sofa and just stared at Justin lying on his daybed. I couldn't imagine putting this little boy through that surgery. It would be extremely painful, and he would not understand what was happening to him. As I sat there, I noticed this large teddy bear that sat at the foot of Justin's bed. It was the ugliest teddy bear he had. The bear had an oversized head and sat up. It wasn't soft and cuddly like most bears and that was its superpower. It felt like a lightbulb went off in my head. I walked over to Justin's bed and put him on his back, which he usually didn't like. I took the bear and placed it between his legs. His legs fit comfortably over the shoulders of the bear. The oversized head offered gentle support between his legs. We began putting him in this position every day. Eventually, the hump on his back disappeared and we never had a problem with his hygiene care. Once I figured out that we had solved a problem and averted surgery, I was upset that the surgeon didn't suggest something like this solution. Joe reminded me that the surgeon wouldn't make any money from solutions that didn't involve surgery. I'm not sure how these doctors sleep at night.

While we were heading to that doctor's appointment, we encountered an extremely rude woman. We were in the lobby of the medical building pushing Justin in his wheelchair toward the elevator. The elevator door was open and there was just enough room for the three of us. The people in the elevator saw us and were waiting patiently as we approached. Just as we were about to enter the elevator, a woman ran in front of us and cut us off. She stepped onto the elevator leaving too little room for us. We were in shock and couldn't believe what just happened. She looked at us as the door was closing and said to us, "I figured you could take the next one." I was in disbelief and didn't have time to respond before the elevator door closed. Thank goodness I believe in karma, but I really hope she never has to experience what life is like with an extremely handicapped child.

Following Justin's death, Joe struggled. He had been Justin's caregiver for almost 14 years, and his life had revolved around Justin and his schedule. Now that Justin was gone, Joe needed to find out who he was and what he wanted to do. He initially kept himself busy with projects around the house. Eventually he would redo every square inch of the interior. He laid tile and painted every room. One of his outdoor projects included a custom-built shed that looked like it was out of a fairy tale. It was one of my favorite things he ever built, and I was sad to leave it behind when we moved from that house.

One night, while he was at work, Joe noticed a flyer on the bulletin board announcing an "in house" dealer school. It was the last day for registration, and Joe quickly signed up for the class. With the extra time he now had, he could attend the class after his shift at work. The class didn't cost anything, but Joe wouldn't get paid for attending either. Approximately 300 people took the class, but only about 28 made it to the casino floor with a job. Joe was one of them. I wasn't surprised and I was so proud of him.

This was an amazing opportunity since normally someone who wanted to become a dealer would pay several hundred dollars to attend a dealer school. Upon completion, a new dealer would need to work his or her way up in a smaller casino before landing a job in a property on the strip. Most of the starting positions meant part-time work while working another full-time position somewhere else. Part-time work in a smaller casino meant less pay. Most new dealers cannot support themselves or their families while they complete this process; it could take years before a new dealer landed a full-time position on the strip. Because of the in-house dealer school, Joe did not need to go through the normal process. He was fortunate enough to start as a new dealer in a full-time position in one of the largest hotel/casinos in the world. His new position as a dealer provided a significant increase to our income. This was the first of many incidents that reminded us we had a guardian angel watching over us now.

Now it was time for me to get out of the grocery business. I hated my position, but it provided us with all the medical coverage we needed for the kids. This was before Obamacare and the security of not being denied medical insurance for preexisting conditions. When we were first married, Joe's insurance wouldn't cover Justin. While Justin's mother enjoyed a lucrative real estate career, she didn't carry any medical insurance on him either. It was my insurance that covered him. I was bitter for a long time, because I had given up my real estate career that I enjoyed and, out of necessity, I continued working in the grocery store.

I had a couple of customers who worked for the city we lived in. One worked in human resources, and another was a dispatcher in the police department. Both had been encouraging me to apply for a city job. I began looking into the position of a 911 operator (also known as a call taker). The only requirement was the ability to type 45 words per minute. It had been a long time, over 45 years, since I had gotten an A+ in my typing class. I was a bit arrogant and over-confident thinking I would easily pass. I tried over and over but was unable to pass. Not wanting to give up, I signed up for a keyboarding class at our community college. I worked hard and not only passed the course, but with practice, I finally passed the typing test and was ready to apply for the position the next time it was open.

After submitting my application, I had to take a written exam along with all the other applicants. Everyone who scored above a certain level moved on to the next part of the hiring process. I was one of the applicants who got to move on. The next part was a performance test. I had to wear headphones and listen to a practice 911 call. While listening, I had to answer questions regarding the call. I missed passing the test by one point. That made me more determined; I was confident I would pass the next time I took the test.

The next time the job was posted, I made it all the way to the selection interviews and was hired. I was so happy to quit my job in the grocery store and excited for what was to come. The training was hard—I mean really hard. There were lots of tears, but I survived and was finally answering calls on my own. That first night, I could barely believe they were trusting me to handle those calls.

I absolutely loved being a 911 operator. The job was both fun and stressful at the same time. Sometimes it felt as though I was spying on the city. I knew everything that was going on. On more than one occasion, I took some unflattering calls from people I knew. Fortunately, they didn't know who I was when they were speaking to me. There was a couple I knew who were arguing when we received the call. Both parties were on the line, each in a different room in their house. The wife had been drinking quite a bit. While on the line with the two of them, the wife could be heard vomiting. It sounded like she threw up in my ear, and I felt the need to wipe my ear at the end of the call. People often ask me about the most memorable calls I received in dispatch. You might be surprised when I tell you the calls that come to mind involve constipation. One night I received a call from an Asian man. His accent was strong, and I wasn't sure I was understanding him correctly. He was sitting on the toilet while speaking with me and wanted an ambulance dispatched to his house because "it was stuck."

Another dispatcher received a constipation call from the mother of a grown woman. The mother was explaining to the dispatcher that she had tried everything to help her daughter go, even a spoon. You really can't make this stuff up. Upon completing the call, the dispatcher said out loud "Note to self, don't ever accept a dinner invitation to that address."

My next constipation call came from a woman who was asking for an ambulance for her husband because he was in pain from constipation. I could hear her husband in the background. I'm not discounting his pain, but he sounded like a little girl. I made sure the woman was okay with us sending paramedics and an ambulance to her home for constipation. She kept saying, "I know" over and over. I don't think she could believe she was calling 911 for this reason.

One of my other most memorable calls came from a woman whose daughter was lying on the bathroom floor giving birth. I'm not sure why, but baby deliveries were our favorite calls. We never got to see the babies, but it was still a cherished moment when we could hear the baby's first cry through the phone. I was following our protocol and asking the soon-to-be grandmother questions regarding her daughter's labor. Suddenly, the baby was out. The call had progressed rather quickly. I was explaining that the baby's airway needed to be cleared when the new grandmother responded, "Okay, let me put my cigarette down." And just like that, she ruined my magical moment. I couldn't help imagining her holding a beer can in her other hand. Like I said, you can't make this stuff up.

The only negative to the job was that the police department never closes. We worked weekends and holidays. After three-and-a-half years, another job opening in the city caught my attention. It was a customer service specialist in the utility department. The position paid more, and I would have weekends and holidays off. It was a hard decision to leave dispatch, but the new position would improve my family's quality of life.

After applying for and getting the position, I worked there for another three-and-a-half years before I noticed another opening in the police department. It was a position in the evidence vault. It was even more money and still offered weekends and holidays off. Since I missed working in the police department, I was excited to apply for the position. Fortunately, I was hired. Before I left the utility department, I needed to have an exit interview with the head of the department. We had a great relationship and I really liked her. During the interview, I told her, "I'm not sure if you noticed or not, but I really am not a customer service specialist." We both had a good chuckle. She congratulated me on my new position.

Before I returned to the police department, I made the decision to have gastric bypass surgery. Joe and I had been married for 10 years and I had gained a lot of weight. I weighed close to 250 pounds. Although I loved Joe with all my heart, I don't think I ever believed he really loved me. I never felt like I was enough. Looking back, I think I was self-sabotaging myself and our relationship. I was trying to prove that if I got fat, he would leave because he didn't really love me. Even with my weight approaching 250 pounds, Joe would often stare at me and tell me I was beautiful. My theory was wrong. He really did love me regardless of the size of my waist. Now, I was obese, and I needed to do something about it. When I told Joe about the surgery, he said he didn't think I needed it, but would support whatever decision I made. After the surgery, I lost about 75 pounds, and it improved the quality of our lives in so many ways. I was happier; therefore, we were happier. Our sex life improved. We were more active, I looked better, I felt better. Everything was better.

From dating picture to pre-gastric bypass surgery

Now is a good time to point out that even though I had a lot of confidence in my ability to do or accomplish anything I wanted to, I lacked self-esteem. I'm not sure why. I guess I am a walking contradiction. I am a work in progress and will probably always struggle with these issues.

I worked in the evidence vault for the next seven years before retiring at the age of 57. The jobs I held at the police department were without a doubt the best jobs I held as a working adult. I made lifelong friends who I still cherish to this day.

When our youngest son was in middle school, he discovered paintball. I had become concerned with the amount of time he was spending playing video games. Once Joe told me that he and our son were outdoors playing a sport together, I told him that no matter what it took, I supported the investment for our son to participate in his newfound passion. Joe told me I had no idea what I was saying —the sport is quite expensive. However, I thought it would be worth every penny if it kept him off his video games. That's how it began. Once we made the commitment, we made a deal with our son. We told him that if he took care of school, we would take care of paint-ball. I didn't realize it at the time, but this commitment involved out-of-state tournaments and practices that included $50 in paintballs. Our son joined a local traveling paintball team and soon became one of the team's valuable players. We made lifelong friends and embraced the paintball community. It was on one of those paintball trips, that I experienced one of my life's most embarrassing moments. We had traveled to a town about two hours away. The boys played in their tournament all day, and then enjoyed dinner together with the team, as we often did. Our son wanted to hang out with his friends, so Joe and I headed back to our hotel room. We were walking down an extremely long hallway that was totally empty except for the two men walking about 20 feet ahead of us. I'm not sure what I ate, but I couldn't help letting a loud fart escape causing the windows to vibrate as the sound echoed throughout the hallway. The two men turned around and looked because it was so loud. Joe just looked at me in disbelief. He knew the two guys thought it was him. The entire scenario made me start to laugh. As soon as I started laughing, more farts escaped, only this time, it sounded like a machine gun was going off. This only caused me to laugh more. Joe wasn't amused as he knew he was taking the blame. Thank goodness there were only two witnesses to my uncontrollable gas. My poor husband—there's never a dull moment with me.

We were extremely proud when our son graduated from high school 18 months early with high honors. He kept up his end of the deal. His accomplishments made all the traveling and weekend trips worthwhile. My schedule enabled me to travel with our son out of state on my days off while Joe stayed behind working. If there was a tournament, he would use his vacation time so he could attend.

Our son

WITH OUR KIDS getting older and moving out on their own, we found time for ourselves for the first time in our marriage. We became interested in taking ballroom dance lessons. We tried several locations, but were kicked out of each class. The instructors wanted us to dance with other people in the class. We were not interested or comfortable doing this. When we explained that we only wanted to dance with each other, we were told we needed private lessons. We decided that was what we would do. One day, while sitting at an intersection, we noticed a sign that said, "Dance lessons" along with a phone number. I quickly wrote down the number and contacted our new dance instructor. He was a perfect fit for us. We looked forward to our dance class every week. It felt like a date for us. There are some unexpected benefits of dance lessons. We became closer and our dance class became somewhat of foreplay for us. We loved looking into one another eyes while we practiced. I think we both consider our dance classes to be one of the best things we ever invested in. Our favorite dance is swing dancing. If we are out and music starts playing, we don't hesitate to dance. Going to weddings is so much more fun knowing that we can dance instead of just doing our high school bop. At one of Joe's high school reunions, we spent some time on the dance floor. When we took a break, Joe was approached by a skinny blonde he had gone to school with. I watched as she approached him holding her hand out and looking at him with sultry eyes. I didn't say anything. I just watched. As she took Joe's hand and attempted to pull him on the dance floor, Joe gently pulled his hand back and politely told her he only dances with his wife. He didn't care if she was offended. I felt very flattered that he was being so respectful of my feelings. The blonde walked away like a dog with its tail between its legs. I didn't care because her actions were very disrespectful towards me.

CHAPTER 8

*A*fter all our kids were grown, Joe and I decided to become involved with network marketing. We joined a company that just made sense to us. It was exciting, and we quickly rose through the ranks. Through the people we met, we had the opportunity to attend some events aimed towards the profession. The tickets to the events were pricey, but we were offered the privilege to volunteer. Not sure of what we were getting into, we accepted the offer.

We became part of an amazing crew led by Loren Lahav. She was—and continues to be—an incredible friend and mentor. When I first met Loren, I was so impressed with her ability to turn a large group of people who didn't know one another into a well-oiled machine by the end of the day. She is incredible and has an extensive background working with Tony Robbins. If I could use just one word to describe her, it would be firecracker. She's not only one of the hardest-working people I have ever met, she's also one of the most generous. I think her heart is bigger than she is. We are better people because Loren Lahav has been in our lives.

The power couple who put on the events were Eric and Marina Worre. They head up their organizations "Network Marketing Pro" and "The Most Powerful Women in Network Marketing." Eric and

Marina bring together the top producers in the industry to teach the best and the latest practices. They do not promote any specific network marketing company. Their goal is to educate and teach business owners how to grow their businesses and maintain the integrity of the industry. Network marketing is a better industry because of these two amazing individuals. We feel blessed to have been involved with their events. We have also been the recipients of their generosity during one of the most difficult times of our lives. I really don't think they understand the impact they have had on us. They are two of the most influential people we have had the privilege to meet.

I mention all this because the personal development we received while volunteering for these events helped us not just in our business, but in our everyday life. Exposure to these events led Joe and me to the conclusion that the company we had joined was, in fact, not giving us the best training to continue growing our business. The advice and suggestions we received from the business leaders almost cost us our relationships with our adult children. We didn't understand why our kids would not support us. We knew if any of our kids came to us with a new business venture and asked for our support, we would do whatever we could do to support them. This was not their response. We felt heartbroken and betrayed, and I'm sure our kids felt the same.

If we can offer one bit of advice for anyone starting their own business, whether it involves networking marketing or not, do not go after your family for initial support. Your family is the most important asset you have. Your family did not choose to go into business, you did. Protect your family relationships at all costs. Practice your marketing on strangers. You are going to screw things up as you get started and learn, and you do not want to damage your family relationships as you navigate through your learning process. Your success will get your family's attention. If they are interested, they will come to you and want to know more about your business and what you are doing.

We have not made a huge amount of money with our network

marketing business, but the things we have learned along the way have been priceless.

I discovered a new company that had all the components we felt were necessary for creating a successful business. More importantly, we would find out that the company was originally created to fund the family's dream of providing a safe haven for victims of sexual abuse to begin their healing process. Excited, I started my new venture. Proudly, I managed to grow my business to the top 2% of the company.

Joe's favorite saying might be "Don't be afraid to jump and build your parachute on the way down." The Lord knows we have lived our lives multiple times with this attitude, and we've never regretted it.

I think one of the most valuable lessons we learned from our personal development over the years is that regardless of the business or line of work you're involved in, your success is based on your relationships. Before you try to sell someone something, be sure you have put in the time and effort to develop a relationship with them. They may or may not be interested in doing business with you. Someday they may refer someone to you based on your relationship with them. That referral could be even more valuable to you. We are constantly planting seeds and it takes time for those seeds to grow.

CHAPTER 9

*I*t was my 59th birthday. I was looking at Joe when I asked, "Do you know what I want for my birthday next year?" He waited for my response; "I want to be driving out of this town."

That was it—no plan, I just knew I wanted to go. My dream was to discover all the beauty this country has to offer. We would slowly figure out our plan.

Two days later, we were enjoying a morning walk and discussing this grand plan of ours. It was common for Joe to always be on the lookout for critters such as lizards and snakes whenever we took walks in the desert. I knew the creatures were out there; I just didn't feel the need to go poking around to find them.

As we were walking, Joe stopped and told me something was moving in the decorative rock along the walkway, but I didn't see anything. I was a little short and impatient with him as he insisted something was moving in the rocks. I took another look, still could not see anything moving and told him so.

Suddenly, his eyes started rolling back in his head. I persuaded him to get down on his hands and knees so his head would not hit the pavement should he pass out. The episode seemed to pass, and I told him he may have just had a seizure. He thought we needed to go to the hospital. During the drive to the hospital, I began to think this was something serious and so much for our "grand plan." Joe assured me we were still going. I wasn't sure if that was going to be possible, but at least I knew he was all in.

At the emergency room, they admitted Joe and ran every test under the sun. While Joe was resting and watching TV, his room suddenly filled with four or five nurses. They began checking his vitals and monitors. He asked the nurses what was going on, and they explained that his heart rate had dropped to 34 beats per minute. They told him that equaled the heart rate of an NBA player at rest. Joe responded that he was too old, too short and too fat to be an NBA player.

Apparently, Joe's heart rate is naturally low. It's called Bradycardia. We were relieved when all his other tests came back normal. Since they couldn't find anything, they ruled the episode a TIA (mini stroke). There wasn't any damage or any proof he had a TIA. It's more likely that since his heart rate is naturally low, his heart wasn't pumping enough blood through his veins as we were walking. His episode mimicked a TIA. It's been four years without any recurrence.

Just a few weeks later, I received a call from my best friend. Her husband had lost his battle with pancreatic cancer. His initial prognosis had been a life expectancy of two months to two years. His battle lasted just shy of five years.

Upon hearing the news, Joe immediately told me I needed to go be with my friend as she navigated through this loss. I contacted her and asked when she would rather have me come—during the services or after. She chose after.

I made my travel arrangements. Logistically, I needed a place to crash for one night before heading to her place. My older sister was visiting my dad, so his guest room was already taken. I asked if I could crash on the couch. His response—that he would put me up in a nearby hotel—sent me into a spiral and reconfirmed my feelings that I didn't matter. I was absolutely crushed. My sister could stay with him, but I needed to stay at a hotel. Reluctantly, I told him I would figure something else out.

When I told my friend what happened, she told me not to worry. She would pick me up at the airport, and I would stay with her. She hadn't planned to have guests leave in the morning, and the next visitor arrive a few hours later, but we managed. However, the pain from the memory remains.

I enjoyed my time with my best friend, and it was difficult to leave when it was time to return home. I know I was a welcomed distraction as she began navigating this new life without her husband.

It was approximately 24 hours after I got back home that I began to feel ill. I had a three-hour stopover in Chicago where I thought I might have picked up a virus. I could have picked something up during my flight as well. It was August in Las Vegas, and I was shivering uncontrollably one moment, then clammy and sweaty the next. This lasted several days.

A week later, I still wasn't feeling well. I told Joe he needed to take me to the emergency room. When we arrived, the nurses asked me about my symptoms. I knew from my experience as a 911 operator that once I told them I had been clammy and sweaty along with chest pains, they would immediately want to rule out any problems with my heart. My blood was drawn, and we waited patiently for the results.

Finally, a snarky little doctor came in and told us it wasn't my heart. (I already knew that.) He said I had a low white blood count, and I needed to follow up with my primary care physician to rule out leukemia. Wow. We did not see that coming, so much for bedside manner. Joe and I sat there feeling like someone had just punched us in the gut. Other than my annual visits to my gynecologist and breast specialist, I hadn't needed a primary care physician. I was never sick.

We found a new primary care doctor who referred me to my current oncologist. At the conclusion of my first appointment with him, he told me that because of my attitude, I was going to do well. I had no idea what he was referring to but was encouraged by his words. He would order my first bone marrow biopsy—the first step to rule out leukemia. Bone marrow biopsies are not fun. They take an eight-inch needle and drill (with an actual drill) into your hip. The needle goes in above your buttocks in your lower back. They alternate sides each time they perform the procedure.

I hate being put under with anesthesia (I'm sure it's a control thing). They told me the procedure only took ten minutes. I figured I could handle anything for ten minutes. After all, I had given birth four times without any drugs. They numbed the area, and I was awake during the procedure. I couldn't see what they were doing since I was face down. The sound of a drill was a little disconcerting, but I managed. I did fine for my first three biopsies, but I don't know what happened on the fourth one. I almost jumped off the table—it was so painful. It may be that it hit an area where they had biopsied before and that caused the extreme pain, but I never again had one done without complete anesthesia.

The purpose of the bone marrow biopsy was to measure the percentage of "blasts" in my bone marrow. Blasts are white blood cells that never matured. Once white blood cells mature, they go into the blood stream. If they don't mature, they begin to back up in your bone marrow.

The first bone marrow biopsy revealed that my blasts were at 8%. A normal healthy adult has approximately 2% blasts. My blasts were already elevated. They would repeat the bone marrow biopsy in three months. That biopsy came back with my blasts at 15%. The blasts had almost doubled in just three months. At this point my diagnosis became MDS (Myelodysplastic Syndrome).

Here is the definition of MDS from the MDS foundation: Myelodysplastic Syndromes are an often-unrecognized under-diagnosed rare group of bone marrow failure disorders where the body no longer makes enough healthy, normal blood cells in the bone marrow. The disease is also known as a form of blood cancer.

While we were trying to figure out exactly what was going on with my health, I received an invitation from our company to attend a VIP event at its headquarters outside Salt Lake City. It was only offered to those of us who had reached the top 2% of the company. Invitations were sent out randomly using a lottery-type system. If I did not accept the invitation, I didn't know when I would receive another one. Unsure of my health situation, but knowing there was a possibility I had leukemia, I felt I should take advantage of the invitation and go.

Although I was tired, I had an amazing time. We were treated like the "Queens" we are. Everything was top notch, and we felt spoiled. The most memorable thing that I took away from the event was a talk from one of our cofounders, Melanie Huscroft. She was an incredible speaker, and it felt as though she was speaking directly to me. She explained that during our lives we are constantly juggling balls. Each area of our lives is represented by a ball. We all manage our relationships, our children or other members of our family we may be responsible for, our business, our homes and of course, our health. Some of the balls are rubber and some are glass. There will be times in our lives when we find we can no longer juggle all the balls and we will need to let some of them go. They will continue to be there, but they will bounce and be waiting for us when we come back. The other balls are made of glass and must be given attention when needed. If we neglect them and they fall, they will break. We need to know it's okay to give the glass balls the attention they need while the other balls bounce.

Melanie's talk was exactly what I needed to hear. My summary doesn't give her the justice she deserves. Since I knew I could be in for a hard battle, I would need to let my business take a back seat while I made my health a priority. It was going to be difficult to do, but I knew it was going to be necessary if I wanted to get better.

Joe and I did not feel we were getting all the answers we needed, so we made the decision to seek a second opinion from the Mayo Clinic in Phoenix, AZ. Our oldest son had had some issues with his blood platelets and sought treatment there. He raved about the care he received. Before we could discuss our decision with my oncologist, he told us he was going to send us out for a second opinion. At least we were on the same page.

Once we arrived at the Mayo Clinic, I knew we had made the right decision. Everything was so well organized, and the patient care was like nothing we had ever experienced. When we met with our doctor there, he told us most people diagnosed with MDS will ultimately develop leukemia. At the conclusion of my first appointment with him, he said the same words that my oncologist said. "You are going to do well because of your attitude." Again, I did not know what he was referring to, but was encouraged by his words.

Three months later my third bone marrow biopsy revealed my blast percentage had increased to 21%. Once the blast percentage reaches 20% or higher, the diagnosis becomes leukemia.

It didn't seem possible that I was so sick. I suffered from headaches and fatigue, but those symptoms did not seem severe enough for such a potentially fatal disease. The doctor explained my options to us. He said he could put me into remission with chemo, and then we would wait for it to come back, because it will. He would then put me into remission again with chemo. He couldn't tell us how long I would stay in remission or how many times he could put me in remission before the chemo would eventually kill me. He told us the ONLY cure for leukemia was a bone marrow transplant. Once I heard this, I knew we were going to opt for the transplant. I watched my mother live with cancer for 15 years before it eventually took her life. Those 15 years were full of medical appointments and monthly cancer shots along with multiple surgeries to help extend her life. As blessed as we were that she lasted 15 years, it was not a life I wanted. Joe and I had too many plans, and they did not include cancer — I wanted the cure.

The first thing the doctors would need to do is put me in remission. They would also need to locate a suitable donor. The best donors are siblings. I have never been so thankful to have four siblings. The only problem was, I hadn't spoken to three of them since our mother passed away three years earlier. One of the three hadn't spoken with any of us for more than 20 years.

I sent a group text to all four of my siblings, explaining that I had been diagnosed with leukemia and needed a transplant. I asked them for permission to share their contact information with the Mayo Clinic to set up testing for a potential match.

Within an hour, all four responded affirmatively. I remember thinking how proud our mother would be. Although there are times that we may not like one another, it was clear that we all loved each other.

My youngest brother had gone through some of his own medical issues that would prevent him from becoming a donor, so he was not tested. Of the remaining three siblings, one was an exact match. It was my older sister, Jayme, and she agreed to be my donor.

It's rather ironic and comical that she would be my match. The two of us have never gotten along. I describe our personalities as oil and vinegar. If the two of us were in the same room for an hour, there would always be an argument.

Since she was the oldest, I think she felt responsible for the rest of us. She may have felt the need to "boss" or control us. My personality always resists anyone who tries to tell me what to do. When I first learned she was an exact match, I wondered if she would agree to be my donor.

While we were navigating our way through the transplant process, we received news that my father had suffered a stroke on Father's Day. In between her trips to the Mayo Clinic, my sister was also traveling to see our dad. She had so many reasons to legitimately back out of being my donor, but she didn't. I will be forever grateful for her gift of life. She will always be my HERO. Regardless of our past or how we go forward with our relationship, I will always love her with all my heart. I am so proud to call her my sister.

The doctors were able to successfully put me into remission. I would need weekly infusions of a drug called Dacogen to stay in remission until my transplant.

My transplant was scheduled for August 1, 2018, four days after my 60th birthday. We continued to question why I contracted this deadly disease. The best explanation was that the virus I came down with after my trip had injured my bone marrow. My bone marrow never recovered, and that ultimately led to leukemia.

Joe and I had started a plant-based diet a few months prior to my getting sick. Once we knew there was something wrong, Joe began juicing fruits and vegetables for the two of us. We continued the plant-based diet for three years. My blood work continued to show that I was slightly anemic, so we slowly reincorporated some meat to increase the iron in my diet. We started with animal organs since they contain the highest level of iron. Currently we practice the 80-20 rule. Our diet is 80% plant based and 20% meat products. We eat bison since it doesn't contain any hormones or antibiotics. Any fish we eat is wild caught, not farmed.

Before we headed back to the Mayo Clinic for my transplant, we made sure we had CBD tinctures containing THC to use while we were in Phoenix. We researched the use of cannabis while battling cancer and found the THC was beneficial for pain and sleep. Before I was admitted to the hospital, we told my doctor I would be using the CBD/THC drops. We needed him to watch my blood levels and let us know if they dropped or increased to an unacceptable level. If they did, I would cut back on the drops. My doctor had no problem with this. I firmly believe cannabis was beneficial in my treatment and recovery. I continue to use it to this day before I go to sleep every night.

As we prepared for our trip to Phoenix, we had no idea where we would be staying once we got there. The only arrangement we had was a two-week reservation at the hotel on the campus of the Mayo Clinic. Joe was stressing out about not having arrangements ahead of time. I told him we just needed to get there, and we would figure it out. You know, jump and build your parachute on the way down.

As we climbed into the car to travel to the Mayo Clinic, we agreed that there would be no country music played on the radio during our drive as we were both extremely fragile emotionally. We were one country song away from losing it. Joe later shared with me that he wasn't sure whether he would be driving home alone or not. We were traveling to a location away from home and trusting doctors who we didn't know very well. We had to believe that they wouldn't kill me while they were trying to save me. I would be receiving intense chemo (poison) for six days prior to my transplant. They were going to bring me to the brink of death, then bring me back.

There's a good chance that if I had asked more questions, I might not have gone through with the transplant. I only asked what I needed to know to get to the next necessary stage of my treatment. My logic was that if I didn't make it, why did I need to know?

In anticipation of my hair falling out from the intense chemo, we shaved my head the night before I was admitted to the hospital. After Joe shaved my head, he reached up and started shaving his own head. We have a beautiful picture of the two of us with bald heads. This was the one thing that never really bothered me. I never even purchased a wig although our insurance would have covered it.

Beautiful bald heads

AFTER WE ARRIVED IN PHOENIX, Joe used social media to seek out anyone who might have connections with someone who worked for the hotel chain where we were staying. The universe answered. A sister of a friend of a friend worked for the chain. Joe's post led to a friends-and-family rate that was good for two months. This was a significant savings for us and took away a lot of stress. Every little bit helped since Joe was going to be out of work for almost four months.

FMLA would protect his job while he was caring for me, but it did not pay him. We not only needed to maintain our household bills at home, but we also needed to pay for food and housing while in Phoenix.

This was not the only generous person who came forward during this time. We received many gifts and cards containing gift cards that helped with gas and groceries. My best friend sent us a very generous cash gift that helped us with expenses. Another touching gift came from a high school classmate who had been diagnosed with a brain tumor a month following my diagnosis. We were able to FaceTime together, both of us sporting our beautiful bald heads. This amazing woman sent us, not just one—but two—generous checks while she was fighting her own battle. Unfortunately, she lost her battle 18 months after her diagnosis. I will never forget her or her kindness. She was a special soul, and our hearts were shattered when we heard of her passing.

RIP Doreen Moberg Picard 7/30/58-10/21/2019

I had another high school classmate who sent me cards multiple times a week throughout our stay in Phoenix and continued long after we returned home. Her cards reminded me I was not fighting this battle alone. She, along with others, were holding my hand and my heart.

You would think by the level of their generous gifts that these ladies and I had been close friends over the years, but other than my best friend, it was quite the contrary. We had been classmates but never "hung out" together. We knew one another from high school and that was it until we reconnected via social media nearly 40 years later. They are just incredible humans, and I am honored and blessed to call them my friends.

There were others who also came forward. We consider them all our angels. All these people humbled us. Before I was diagnosed with leukemia, Joe and I always felt as though we were on our own. We have always been extremely independent, and it was difficult for us to accept help. Without these generous gifts, I'm not sure we would have survived and remained financially fluid. Their acts of kindness changed us as individuals. We now understand we are not alone. People do care.

The night before I was admitted to the hospital, Joe and I were enjoying our last night together at the hotel. We received a call from the front desk that we had a package. Joe went down and brought back an unbelievably generous gift left anonymously for us. It was a large beautiful wooden chest full of the most thoughtful gifts. The person who left the chest put so much thought into each gift inside. They knew my favorite color, and there were several gift cards that helped immensely. We were amazed by this generosity. We eventually figured out who this angel was, but we don't want to take her anonymity away. She will always be in our hearts.

When it came time to check into the Mayo Clinic, I was very scared. There were several tests and appointments prior to being admitted. I was following instructions and going through the motions each step of the way. When we finally got to my room, I think I realized there was no turning back. The nurses started giving us instructions and explaining the information that would be documented on the white board in my room. When they got to the part about measuring and recording my urine and stool output, I lost it. I stood in the doorway and just bawled. I felt as though I was losing my dignity. They wanted me to notify someone every time I needed to use the bathroom. This was something I was not willing to do; I had to have control over this one thing. The nurses knew I was not budging, and we finally agreed on a compromise. Joe would be my bath-room buddy (lucky him) and would document the information on the white board. This was true love and just one of the endless things this man did and continues to do to this day. (No, he doesn't need to go to the bathroom with me any longer, but you know what I mean.)

After six days of intense chemo, followed by one day off, I received the donated stem cells from my sister. She was in a nearby room hooked up to a machine that took the cells from her and spun them. This process enabled them to determine which cells they needed. Once enough cells were collected, the bag was brought into my room. It was hung on an IV pole and infused into my body through a port that had been surgically implanted in my chest. The total infusion took approximately an hour. It was rather anticlimactic.

My Hero

Little did I know, that was the easy part. The effects from the intense chemo hadn't even begun. My white blood count was drop-ping and would continue to decline. My immune system no longer existed. If I caught a cold or any type of virus, it would most likely kill me. It would take 16 days before my numbers would start to go up. During this time, I developed white sores in my mouth that were extremely painful. It hurt to eat, drink or swallow. All I wanted to do was sleep—hoping that when I woke up, it would all be over.

One night Joe found himself questioning our decision to go forward with the transplant. It had been a rough day for me, and he was having a difficult time watching me suffer. As he was walking, he noticed a rock. He picked it up and it had a message on it—keep the faith. That rock gave him reassurance and hope. Joe continued to find rocks with inspirational quotes and sayings on them. These rocks gave him strength and brightened his days. This continued almost the entire time we were in Phoenix. If you have ever come across a painted rock with a message on it, you might understand. We collected about 50 rocks during our stay. We started leaving them for other people since we knew the effect they were having on us. Joe still has the original rock, though.

Even when I was having a rough day and having a difficult time finding the strength and energy to get out of bed, the doctors had other plans. Regardless of how bad I felt, they wanted me to get up and walk around the hospital floor.

Each patient's room on our wing had a separate door to enter the room and another door to exit the room. This was supposed to reduce the circulation of the outside air coming into each room. The number of precautions taken to keep each patient safe in this environment was quite impressive. I felt very safe despite my condition.

At one point I refused to get up and walk. I just wanted to sleep and told everyone so. Joe became very concerned, as did the doctors. I was later told they thought they were losing me. Joe made a call to our oldest son asking him to come to Phoenix. Joe knew our son would persuade me to get up and walk. He was right. Joe understood that I wanted my kids to be proud of the way I battled this disease, and he was counting on the bond that my son and I shared. It only took my son about 20 minutes to get me up and walking.

Sometime during the 16 days following my transplant, my brother and sister-in-law visited me in the hospital. I think they also brought us a new supply of CBD/THC drops. It would be weeks before I realized they had visited me.

My numbers continued to improve indicating the transplant was working. The days following my transplant were the most difficult. Sometimes I felt it would be easier to die than continue fighting. The one thing that kept me going was watching how hard Joe was working to keep me alive. I couldn't give up while watching him fight for me.

When the pain became unbearable, I would ask Joe to take me on a trip. I would lie back in my hospital bed and close my eyes while he would talk me through an imaginary trip. I remember him telling me we were driving up the Pacific Coast Highway in California. He described everything we would see. It was our dream of traveling together that kept me fighting. I knew I had to get better so we could fulfill this dream.

Our nurse witnessed one of our imaginary trips. We also told her about one of our favorite YouTube families who were traveling full time with their three kids. She went home and started watching them and was immediately hooked. She began binge watching to catch up on all their seasons.

Tara, decided to reach out to the YouTube couple—Marc and Trish Leach. Their channel is called Keep Your Daydream or KYD. Tara told them about us and explained how we had shared their channel with her. She knew that their home base was Phoenix. They were just finishing a trip to Alaska and would be back in Phoenix soon. Tara asked them if there was any way we could have a "meetup" with them once they returned home. Without hesitation, they agreed. All the arrangements were made without our knowledge, but HIPPA laws meant Tara needed to bring Joe in on the plans.

Once I was released from the hospital, I still needed to return twice a week to have my blood levels checked. It was during one of these visits, that I was surprised. My younger daughter, Casey was with us that day. I had been told that I had a surprise visitor coming but had no idea who it was. After my blood had been drawn and we were waiting for the results, Joe told me he needed to use the restroom. He left the room; he had just received a text from Tara. I hadn't seen Tara since I was discharged from the hospital, so I was beyond excited when she came back to the room with Joe. I gave her a huge hug and was pleased that she was my surprise. While I was squealing with joy, a petite beautiful blonde peeked through the door. I immediately recognized Trish and her handsome redheaded husband, Marc, standing behind her. I looked at Joe and asked him how he did this. He shook his head and pointed to Tara, indicating she was the one who had organized the surprise.

Marc and Trish visited with us for almost two hours. They were exactly as they appeared on their YouTube channel videos — authentic and genuine. We will never forget their kindness and generosity with their time. You can check out the surprise on their YouTube channel @keepyourdaydream. It's the final episode of their season five.

Joe, Casey, Tara, Trish, Carrie and Marc

Not long after that, we returned home. I came back almost 50 pounds lighter and with no hair. I'm sure my little grandsons were concerned by my appearance. I was no longer the person they said goodbye to almost four months earlier. It was difficult to come to terms with the idea that I would never be that person again. My life would now be defined by "before leukemia" and "after leukemia." There was absolutely nothing about my body that would ever be the same. The physical differences were obvious; the things people couldn't see were endless. Foods that I couldn't eat or wanted to eat had changed. Emotionally, I was permanently scarred. My reactions to situations were and still are, rather unpredictable. My frustration level is extremely low. Joe frequently hears me "growling" when something doesn't go my way. All he wants to do is fix it for me and sometimes he just can't. He's learning to let me work my way through situations. Sometimes I'm not very pleasant to be around. When this happens, I usually feel remorse and start crying. After everything Joe has gone through with me, I hate when I make his life more difficult. When he is understanding, I feel even worse. A country music song could and still can start the water works. The response from friends and family was overwhelming. I have never felt more loved. Joe was beyond grateful that he didn't have to make the trip home alone.

Before we headed back to Vegas, we had the opportunity to enjoy the Arizona State Fair. It was the largest fair we have ever attended. While we were there, we found an artist who did henna tattoos. I asked her to do my bald head. She was happy to oblige. I showed her a picture of one of the rocks I had painted, and she used it as inspiration. I loved it and only wished it lasted longer. It stayed on my head for almost two weeks.

One of the things I found interesting as I went out into the world with a bald head is the way people treated me. I noticed how nice people were when you are bald. It's probably because we all know someone who has gone through some sort of cancer battle, and the bald head is a badge of honor for some. It symbolizes that you are still in the fight. People have compassion and wish you well. That behavior starts to change as your hair begins to grow back. When my hair was between a bald head and a chosen style, it seemed as though people weren't as open minded. During this time, I would make sure Joe held my hand while we were in public. I didn't do this out of shame or embarrassment; I did it because I didn't want to deal with close-minded people.

My Henna tattoo

There are not enough pages in this book for me to adequately share the love and care Joe demonstrated during my entire illness. It continues to this day. Not a day goes by that he doesn't ask me if I'm okay or if I need anything. I remember Joe holding my face in his hands with tears running down his cheeks, wishing out loud that it was him rather than me going through this battle. Eventually I needed to tell him to stop doing everything for me because it made me feel like I was still sick. I love him for wanting to though.

My favorite spot in the entire world is when I place my head on his chest. It fits perfectly and my heart is full. It's my safe place. I know, without a doubt, he would do anything and everything to keep me alive. If I had just one wish, it would be that everyone could know what it is like to be loved like this.

This past year I happened to come across a social media post that announced that Marc and Trish were going to be speaking at a local event here in Vegas. In fact, the property where they were speaking was only five minutes from where we are currently staying. I was on a mission to see them. Lovingly, I persuaded Joe to come along to help me surprise them. He didn't believe we could get close to them.

We had worked enough events to know how they are run, and I was sure we could get in and get close enough to them.

We headed to the venue dressed in our logo shirts, so we looked like we belonged in the crowd. We had shirts and hats made with the name of our YouTube channel, Facebook page and Instagram account. They come in handy when attending events or starting conversations when we are out and about. If someone questioned us at the event we were crashing, I was ready to tell them we were guest speakers. We had no trouble walking into the local venue where Marc and Trish were supposed to be. Joe was loaded up with all his camera gear, so he looked official. We walked around and visited the vendors as I continued to scan the crowd looking for Marc and Trish. The audio-visual area was always a good place to check, and I was so excited when I caught a glimpse of Marc. Filled with excitement, I grabbed Joe and told him to follow me. We approached Marc, and he immediately remembered us. He called out to Trish who was behind a curtain in a nearby section. She came out to greet us and was equally surprised. They couldn't believe we were there, because we were going to be mentioned in their speech regarding people we meet while living the RV lifestyle. They invited us to stay since they were the first ones scheduled to speak. We enjoyed surprising them and were flattered that they asked us to stay. We love following them and look forward to crossing paths again in the future.

When we returned home from the Mayo Clinic, I was amazed at

how much my muscles had atrophied. My legs were very weak. Things that you never think about were now a challenge. Getting up off the toilet took every bit of strength I had. I usually braced myself using the toilet paper holder. I couldn't take off my jeans without sitting down and I couldn't balance myself putting them on. It's a good thing we had a bench seat in our shower because I would frequently need to sit down while showering. Fortunately, I no longer had hair on my legs, so shaving was not an issue. That lasted about a year before it started growing back. The thing that helped me most to regain my strength was my little dog, Younique. We have never owned a dog that loved going for walks as much as she does. Because of her, I walked (and still walk) about a mile every day and slowly my strength has increased. She's my motivation and without her, I'm sure I wouldn't be as diligent about walking.

Joe and Younique

CHAPTER 10

*I*n the preface of this book, I mention that the motivation to write came from my mother. That is only partially true. For almost 30 years, I have been relentless in encouraging Joe to write this book. His strength has always inspired me, and I knew his story could inspire someone else. I finally gave up and decided to write it myself. After I began writing, and put the abuse Joe suffered into words, I had to apologize to him. It was extremely difficult to describe the stories he had shared with me. I told him how sorry I was to have thought he could go to those very dark experiences and share them with the world. Tears were running down my face as I wrote that chapter. Shame on me for thinking he could relive those experiences and put them into print. Thankfully he gave me permission to include them in my book.

Every time I look at my husband, I cherish him for the man he is. It was his smile and beautiful green eyes that attracted me when we first met. I never saw him without a smile. He has an infectious energy. If Joe walks into the room, you know he is there. I don't think there is anything in his background that could explain how he became the exceptional human that he is.

Although he loved his father, he would agree that his dad was not a very good husband. One example presented itself early in our marriage. We were at his parents' house, and his father was sitting on the sofa watching the oversized TV. Joe's dad was legally blind, and the large screen allowed him to see more easily. Joe's mother was busy cooking in the kitchen, which was adjacent to the TV room. Joe and I were sitting between the two rooms. At one point, Joe's dad called out his mom's name. She didn't answer or respond. He called her again. Still no answer. After the third time, his mother stopped what she was doing and walked to where his dad was sitting. He told her to change the TV channel. I couldn't believe it. First, he had the remote next to him. It was an oversized remote so he could easily maneuver it. Second, Joe and I were sitting there doing nothing. We could have changed it for him. As I witnessed this behavior and realized what was taking place, I gave Joe a look that needed no words. My expression was clear—loud and clear. He knew I was saying, "Don't you ever think about treating me that way!"

I'm sure it was part of their culture, but it was not mine. When Joe's dad was dying, most of his 11 remaining siblings came to see him. Their house was full of relatives. All the women were in the kitchen cooking. All the brothers were sitting in chairs around the table with their arms folded across their chests just waiting for the women to serve them. The aunts saw me and invited me into the kitchen. I appreciated that they wanted to include me, but there was no way I was interested in waiting on these men who I didn't really know. In my world, the men took care of the women or at least shared the workload. My dad taught me that. I politely declined their invitation.

With all the relatives visiting, I was the only one in the house who was not of Mexican descent. Fortunately, there was at least one aunt and one cousin who approved of me. It was obvious that the others considered me an outsider, and I was okay with that. It didn't bother me. During this time, Joe and I were dealing with the knowledge that his mother was an incestuous pedophiliac rapist. In my mind she should be prosecuted and jailed for what she did to her little boy, but I can't imagine what that would be like for Joe should he decide to press charges against her. He would have to testify in court and describe his abuse publicly. She was a monster, but she was still his mother. He has survived her abuse, but he would need to relive it repeatedly to have her prosecuted. As much as she deserves to be criminally charged, I can't imagine the embarrassment and shame Joe would have to endure to bring her to justice. He has been extremely open regarding his abuse, but he doesn't want to be regarded as the guy who was sexually abused by his mother. He is so much more than that. She doesn't get to torment him any longer.

Before Joe moved out of his parents' house, he told me about a day he was in their bedroom putting away some clean laundry. As he worked, his foot rubbed up against a paper bag under the bed. His curiosity got the best of him, and he pulled the bag out to see the contents. I can't imagine the emotions he felt when he discovered the artificial penis with leather straps. Yes, it was the same device she wore when she raped him years earlier as a little boy. I often wonder why she would even own such a thing, especially after all these years, and then I must change channels in my brain, because I don't want to go there.

I once witnessed Joe's oldest brother say out loud that he hadn't met a woman who he would let wipe off his shoes. Not surprisingly, he is still single. This was the big brother that Joe looked up to as a little boy. I am so grateful he did not take on the same mentality as his brother. By the grace of God, Joe has the complete opposite opinion of women.

With his culture, and the male examples in his life, I still wonder how Joe turned out to be such an amazing husband. Early on in our relationship, I started to realize how different I felt when I was with him. Whenever I was with someone prior to Joe, I constantly heard the little voices in my head. The voices continually asked me who I needed to be for someone to love me. When I looked in the mirror, I wondered if I was pretty or thin enough. I felt anxious and uncomfortable with who I was. I was always trying too hard to be someone

I wasn't. When I was with Joe, I noticed all those feelings went away. He liked me just the way I was—all of me. I have never felt that way with anyone.

I know our relationship is rare. We both acknowledge that. From our story, you know life has been both difficult and challenging at times. A lot of the things we have survived would have destroyed other relationships. I believe they have only strengthened ours. We have grown together and become who we are today because of everything we have been through. I don't think we would change a thing, because we both like who we are today. We have spent half our lives with one another, which is considerably longer than we spent with our parents or kids.

Over the years, I have asked Joe if he met the old me today, would he marry me. His response continues to be, "No." I think of the old Joe and know that the person I am today would not marry that version of him either.

Despite all the hardships we have endured, we have no problem finding humor in everyday experiences. Or perhaps, because of the hardships, we have developed a sick sense of humor. Regardless, it's not hard to find ourselves laughing at the silliest things. One day we went to the movie theater located inside one of our local hotel/casinos. As we were heading towards the doors to leave the casino, Joe asked me if I wanted to "invest 20" That is code for "Do you want to gamble?" I responded with, "Sure." In front of us and just to the left of the exit doors, was a bank of five video poker machines. There were two empty spots and Joe asked me if I wanted the one on the right or the left. I took the one on the right. We started playing and I noticed a strong body odor coming from the gentleman sitting to my right. Every time someone would come through the doors, it would blow some air our way, and I could smell it. I was sitting there with my shirt pulled up over my nose to buffer the smell. Joe asked me what was wrong, and I explained. He asked if I wanted to leave or go to other machines. I told him my machine was playing well, and I didn't want to leave. We continued playing. The person on the far right lit up a cigarette. The woman to the left of Joe started complaining out loud, saying it had been so nice because there hadn't been any smokers around. Joe told her that the smoke might be a relief because the guy sitting next to me had bad body odor. The lady finished playing her machine and walked over to her husband, who happened to be the guy with the body odor. Joe and I just sat there looking straight ahead. When the couple left, Joe and I said, "We are going to hell."

There isn't anyone I would rather spend time with than Joe. We both have a difficult time when he goes to work. His days off are our favorite days. We really are best friends. No one gets me like he does. Like I mentioned, we find humor in everyday situations. Having someone in your life that can bring you to tears from laughing so hard is a priceless gift. It's one of the things I value most about our relationship. Laughing at a situation is much better than crying over it, although we've done our fair share of both.

I have never met anyone who works as hard as Joe. He has always amazed me. Over the years, I don't believe I have ever seen him sleep a full eight hours. He usually exists on four to five hours of sleep. The thing that bothers me most is that he always puts himself last. He has a difficult time spending money on things he likes. I usually must insist he buy something for himself. We have finally reached the age where he will reluctantly pay someone to do something he could do but might get injured doing. It's only when I remind him that our future could disappear if he got hurt then he acquiesces. Just the other day, he sprained his ankle walking around outside on the uneven grass. It sucks getting old, but we appreciate the privilege. So many people we know have died much too young.

It's a gift knowing Joe always has my back. We make a great team. When one of us is struggling, the other always steps up. We do have our strengths and weaknesses. Together, we agree that Joe is a much better caregiver than he is a patient, and I am a better patient than caregiver (but I am working on the caregiver part).

This amazing journey, that we call life, has taught us some important lessons. We have learned through personal experiences and personal development. Both have been valuable. One of my favorite quotes comes from Henry Ford. He wisely said, "If you think you can or you think you can't, you're right."

One of the most valuable lessons we learned early in our marriage counseling was people will treat you the way you let them. They will not stop doing what they are doing until you stop what you are doing, and that is letting them get away with it. This lesson not only helped our marriage, but it also helped with all our relationships —family and friends. If we find ourselves stressed out or offended by someone's behavior, and we have made it clear that it is unacceptable, we have no problem distancing ourselves regardless of who it is. We have learned that even when you love someone, sometimes you must love them from a distance.

One of my favorite discoveries over the years was learning that what other people think of us is none of our business. We don't live our lives based on other people's opinions. We realize most people would not make the decisions we have, and that's okay. When we plan, it's based on what will make us happy, not what other people think.

We have learned not to live our lives in fear. We refuse to create our future based on fear. In fact, if it's not a little scary, then what's the point in doing it? It adds to the excitement.

When Joe sometimes stresses out over something we are dealing with, I gently remind him that we didn't have to bury a child that day, so we are going to be all right. We have already survived the worst thing a parent could go through, so we know we can survive whatever comes our way.

We are all going to experience things that will literally bring us to our knees. How we handle those things will determine our future happiness. We have never asked, "Why us?" Really, why not us? We refuse to play the victim. We find strength in one another and take the lesson, whatever it may be, and grow from it.

Without Joe's love and support, I know I would not be here. My sister is my hero, and the doctors worked their magic, but if I did not see everything Joe was doing to keep me alive, I would not have had it in me to fight through the hardest part of my battle with leukemia.

I remember lying in my hospital bed thinking it would be easier to die instead of continuing the battle, but I knew I couldn't stop fighting if Joe was there beside me. Knowing there isn't anything this man wouldn't do to keep me alive is what gave me the strength to push through the pain. To say I am completely and totally in love with this man is an understatement. As hard as I try, I don't have the words to express the love I have for him. All I know is that I have been blessed to share this life with him.

The most recent lesson we have learned came during the holiday season. I'm not sure what triggered it—maybe it was COVID exhaustion. We found ourselves very depressed and it was difficult to shake. I finally heard something that got us out of it. I heard we should not focus on what we have lost or what we don't have. We should focus on what we do have and the people in our lives who we enjoy spending time with. Just switching our thoughts helped bring us out of it. We all have people we know who bring us down and those who bring us energy. We get to choose who we spend our precious time with. If you are around someone who drains your energy because their lives are full of drama, it might be in your best interest to limit your time with them. We like to be with people who we look forward to seeing again as soon as we leave them.

When we completed marriage and family therapy, our therapist told us we had the equivalent of a master's degree in family functions. She is responsible for not only saving our marriage, but also saving our lives. We were devastated when we recently heard of her passing. I hope we can honor her by continuing to use every skill she taught us and keeping our relationship strong.

Through our therapy, we learned that regardless of where we are in our lives, we all need to realize that we are there because of the choices we have made. We are responsible, and it doesn't serve any purpose to blame a situation or a person for things that happen to us. We can think back and recognize the decisions that brought us to our current situation. We also need to recognize that if we don't like where we are, we have the power to change it.

I thank God that I am still here to write this book. I pray that we have many more years together with more stories to share. My hope is that we meet enough future friends who want to share their stories and I can write another book, or maybe two!

Joe and I

*PHOTO CREDIT JULIANA GOLDBERG

MY MOM

*I*t was the year 2000, and I was working in dispatch as a 911 operator when I received the call from my dad informing me that my mother had been diagnosed with cancer. While quietly crying, I tried to keep enough composure to handle the calls coming in even as I tried to process the news. We didn't know a lot about her cancer, except it was rare and slow moving. I believe it was called a carcinoid cancer. Those two characteristics made it possible for her to live with the cancer for 15 years after her diagnosis. Instead of traveling and enjoying their retirement, my parents' lives involved endless medical appointments, treatments and surgeries. One of her surgeries was the equivalent of seven procedures. She had an amazing surgeon who knew she would never survive seven individual procedures, so she took the risk and completed them all at one time. It was a bold move on her part, and we are so grateful for her skills because she probably extended my mother's life another five years. My mother was tiny, but tough. She recovered beautifully.

The doctors had to finally tell my mother that they had done everything within their power and there was nothing further they could do. This was December of 2014. When I received the call from my parents, I told Joe I needed to go and be with my mother. Fortunately, I had recently retired, so I was able to purchase a one-way ticket to Maine to spend whatever time she had left with her. I wasn't looking forward to the cold winter, but it didn't matter. I needed to be there.

When I arrived in Maine, I initially stayed at my younger sister's house. We were only five minutes from my parents' home. My mom didn't appear to be at the end of her life. Her condition allowed us to spend some quality time with her before she began to deteriorate. My brother Jim also joined us in Maine. Most of my mom's grandkids were able to visit her while she could still enjoy them.

Slowly her condition worsened. She began having difficulty getting to the bathroom. First, there was a potty chair, so she could just get out of bed, take a couple of steps and then get back in bed. She collapsed on the floor early one morning and my dad had to call the paramedics to help get her off the floor. Early one morning, we received a phone call from our dad, asking when we would be over. He told us we didn't need to hurry, but our mother was having difficulty getting back into bed after using the toilet. When we arrived, we found my mother face down on the edge of her bed. Her pants were around her ankles because my dad couldn't get them back up. He had placed a small towel on her behind for modesty. I was able to gently get her back in bed. We don't really know how long she had been lying there like that. She did not have the strength to stand and get back in bed. My father told her to just dive towards the bed. She made a valiant attempt, but only made it to the edge, face down. Every time my dad tried to help her move, his hands hurt her, and she cried out in pain.

We needed to make new arrangements. Fortunately, my mother's hospice nurse told my dad he could no longer stay alone with my mother. We had been trying to get him to allow us to sleep at his house, but he had been adamant that he didn't want us there. He no longer had a choice; if he wanted to keep her at home, someone else needed to be there. We ordered a hospital bed to replace the sofa she used during the day, and she began using a bedpan to reduce the chances of her falling again.

On the day the hospital bed was scheduled for delivery, there was a huge snowstorm. To get to my parents' house early in the morning, we had to shovel my sister's walkway and driveway before we left. When we arrived at my parents', we needed to shovel a pathway so the bed could be delivered. It was extremely cold and still snowing. My brother Jim had returned home, and it was only my sister and me. Things were getting overwhelming. I found my sister in the back yard digging her way to my parents' satellite dish. The dish was full of snow and the TV had no reception. She knew watching television was all they had to do all day, so she was determined to clear the dish. Tears were running down her face as she dug through the snow. Everything was hard, and the weather made it even harder.

The most traumatic day for me was the day my brother Jim needed to leave and return home. I was standing in the kitchen of my parent's small home, and my brother had gone into the bedroom to say his final goodbye to my mom. He knew he would never see her alive again. He stepped out of her bedroom and nearly collapsed on the floor. He was filled with grief and sobbing. There was nothing anyone could do to console him, and we all knew we would be experiencing the same grief soon. I will never forget that moment. Just the memory brings so much sorrow and pain. Witnessing this made me realize I could not leave my mom knowing I was never going to see her alive again. It was such a blessing that retirement allowed me to focus on my mother and spend every last precious moment with her.

Watching my brother sob with grief brought back a memory of him starting kindergarten. He was young starting school and was not ready to leave my mom. When it was time for him to go inside the school, he panicked and started screaming in fear. He wasn't weeping, he was traumatized and you could tell by the sound of his cries. As the teacher picked him up to carry him inside, his cries intensified. With my brother in her arms, the teacher walked around the corner of the building. My brother grabbed the corner of the brick building in an attempt to prevent the teacher from bringing him inside. As I witnessed this, I began to cry as well. I wanted to save my little brother but I was helpless. Fortunately, my parents and the teachers all agreed that my little brother was not ready to leave my mom. Thank goodness they decided to keep him out of school one more year. That allowed him to be in the same class as my youngest brother, which would hopefully be less traumatic for him. Watching him cry and grieve after walking out of my mother's bedroom brought back those traumatic memories.

There was so much snow, that when my oldest son and my nephew arrived, they had to remove it from the roof. We were worried about the weight on the roof of my parents' small house. The two boys were outside in the freezing cold without the proper clothing, but wouldn't stop until the job was done. Next my dad's automatic garage door stopped working. The boys spent hours out in the cold trying to fix it. They needed to call my brother, Jim, in Vegas to get his help and guidance. They sent him pictures and face-timed him so he could talk them through the repair. Together they were successful, and my dad was extremely grateful.

One day while my mom was still able to speak, I was giving her a sponge bath. She asked me if I ever thought I would be taking care of and bathing her. I asked her if there was someone else she'd rather have do it. She told me no. It was a blessing to be able to be there, and I told her so. It was life coming full circle. She used to bathe me as a child and now I was doing the same for her. Our family has always been extremely modest, so I knew it was difficult for my mother to have someone bathe her—even if it was her daughter. I will never forget those precious moments.

The last time my mother made me laugh out loud was shortly before she died. My sister Tammy, my brother Jim and I arrived at my parents' house one morning. When we walked in, my mother said to us "Oh, now you're here." She told us she saw a deal on TV for 25 pounds of M&Ms. We started laughing and asked her if she knew what 25 pounds of M&Ms looked like. She told us to never mind because she wasn't sure she would like them anyway because they were pastel colored. We started laughing again and told her all M&Ms tasted the same. She insisted they did not. She said the different colors were different flavors. We all had a good laugh and I always smile when I see M&Ms. At her memorial service I had pastel

M&Ms made with all her names on them. Some said Mom, some said Peggy or Nanny, and some said Doris, which was her given name. I handed the little bundles of M&M's to everyone in attendance. I also painted a rock like a pink M&M, and I keep it next to my bed.

My mother passed February 15, 2015. That day, my oldest son, Nick was there with me, along with my niece, Danielle, and her brother James. My sisters and my dad were all there as well. My son and nephew are both firefighter/paramedics. We all knew the end was near. My mother was no longer conscious and could not communicate with us. Her breathing was changing. We were all sitting around her hospital bed in the living room. I remember watching her breaths became slower and slower. I could feel myself physically trying to help her breathe as my chest rose and my lungs filled with air. I didn't want her to stop breathing, but I didn't want her to suffer any longer either. Eventually, she took her last breath. Without any conversation, my dad just looked at my son and nodded. He instinctively knew what his role was. He walked over to my mom, checked her pulse and called out her time of death. I will never forget that moment as long as I live. My son probably never expected to perform that role on his grandmother when he began his career, but he was the perfect person to do it. He was her first-born grandson after all.

As you can imagine, we were all extremely emotional. Each of us was trying to deal with the loss in our own way. We asked our dad if he wanted us to call the coroner. To our surprise, he didn't. He wanted to keep her body overnight at the house with him. We tried to tell him he was "batshit crazy," but ultimately, since he wasn't hurting anyone, so we didn't interfere. I did, however, explain that he couldn't have a dead body lying in his living room unless he allowed me to clean her up. If you don't know, when someone dies, all their body fluids exit the body. My sister Jayme assisted me. She was a little reluctant at first, and she continually gagged during the process, but we managed to get the job done. I'm sure my experience taking care of Justin prepared me for this day.

My sister Tammy stayed the night with my dad. The following morning, I sent her a text asking her how it was going. She replied that she was having coffee with my mom and dad, and I told her I would be right over. I couldn't miss this. My dad was finally able to pull the sheet over my mom and give us permission to call the coroner. After the coroner left with my mom, my father explained why he kept her body overnight. He told us that my mother hated to be cold, and he didn't want her lying alone in the morgue until someone got there. He knew she would be cold. None of this made sense, but it was so sweet to know that he was still looking out for her. In his mind, he was protecting her.

Losing my mother is without a doubt the most painful loss I have experienced. It's been seven years, and the pain is as strong as it was that day. I miss her more than I knew was possible. Tears run down my face as I thank God for giving her to me. My siblings and I were so blessed because she was our mom. I loved my dad, but not the way I loved my mom. I was fortunate to be the only daughter who consistently lived in Vegas during the time my parents lived here. My sisters lived in Vegas for short periods of time, and they would visit, but I was able to spend most of my adult life living in the same area with my parents until they returned to Maine. Those years gave me precious time with my mom and our relationship was very close. For years I enjoyed weekly lunches with my mom, her mom and several of her sisters. When my dad retired and they moved back to Maine, my mother and I would enjoy weekly phone calls, usually every Sunday. She may be gone, but these memories remain in my heart.

It was difficult to call my dad after my mom died. I knew I should call, but I didn't want to. I was angry that my mother was the one who was gone. She was the one I always wanted to talk to. On the days I would call, my dad would almost always answer the phone. After a quick hello, I would ask to speak with my mother. My father has always been the one to "fix" things for us. He just didn't know what to do if we wanted to talk to him about "feelings." If we had a problem that he could help us fix, he was there for us, but if it involved our feelings, he didn't know what to do. It must have been difficult for my mother to discuss her feelings with him. When I was young, I thought my dad was my "knight in shining armor." As I got older and discovered more mature relationships, I often asked my mother how she could stay married to him. Seeing him through adult eyes, changed my perspective of him.

He did a good job providing for our family and taking care of my mother. He left home at 17 and went into the Navy. He grew up quickly and I know his parents were strict with him. My curiosity led me to ask him why he wanted to marry my mom. He told me it was because he was horny. Knowing that he grew up in the Catholic Church, it made sense—not very romantic, but logical. If he wanted to have sex, they needed to be married first. I'm sure he was a little disappointed on his wedding night because my mother had never been told about sex. You would think with four sisters, one of them might have given her the "talk" before her wedding night. I can't imagine what my father was thinking when my mother asked him, "You want to put that where?" She was so frightened that she proceeded to get drunk and hugged the toilet all night long. Together they must have figured things out. They did have five children after all, although I think she was pregnant with my younger sister before she realized what was causing the pregnancies. After the youngest

117

was born, the doctor came out of the delivery room and told my dad if he got my mother pregnant again, he would be raising six children by himself. Her last pregnancy almost killed her.

Since no one had the "talk" with my mother, she didn't know enough to talk to her daughters. I remember walking into my mom's bedroom when my older sister had started her period. My mother was forced to talk to her about it, because my sister thought she was dying. It's a good thing I walked in on them, because I started my period the following week. At least it wasn't as traumatic for me.

Following my mother's death, I found myself lost. My heart had a hole in it and getting up every day was difficult. My mother knew I had been gifted with artistic abilities and she had expressed her disappointment that I was not using those skills. Now, that I was no longer busy raising young children, I accepted her nudging and started painting rocks. I'm not sure what intrigued me about painting rocks, but it was a wonderful distraction as I navigated this loss. The work was very detailed and focusing on the design kept my mind off losing my mother. If I have gifted you one of these rocks, you have a special place in my heart.

One of my painted rocks

TIME HASN'T MADE the loss of my mother any easier. It's just different. I have cried more tears over losing my mom than any other loss I have experienced. Knowing how painful it was going to be, I waited to write this chapter until last. As time has passed, I've tried to turn the pain into gratitude. I remind myself how blessed I am to have had her as my mother.

Dear Mom, I did it!

My mom

EPILOGUE

*a*s I wrote this book and began sharing memories and experiences, I found myself laughing and crying as if they had just happened. It is my hope that the stories trigger some emotions for you. If you know people who have overcome tragedy and loss or been a survivor, maybe you can share the book with them. You never know where they are in their recovery. While reading this book, I hope you found some humor, inspiration and value in it.

A year ago, we sold our large home and got rid of everything in it. We purchased an RV where we are currently living. Joe is still working towards his retirement while we figure out our health insurance and patiently wait for gas prices to come down before we start our travels. This past year, we have been primarily stationary in our local RV resort. I wasn't sure I was going to like it because I thought it might feel as though we were living in a parking lot. Surprisingly, we have enjoyed this resort and have made some lifelong friends. We found that RV people are some of the friendliest people around, and the relationships we have formed exceed any friendships we made during the ten years living in our previous neighborhood.

One of those relationships began in the community pool. Joe and

I were enjoying ourselves in the pool when I overheard a conversation between two ladies. I wasn't trying to listen in, but I couldn't help but hear part of the conversation. One lady, who I would find out was named Katy, was sharing with the other lady that she found out the hard way that vanilla doesn't go well in eggs. As soon as I heard her make that statement, I began laughing out loud. After apologizing and explaining that I wasn't trying to listen in on their conversation, we had a good chuckle as she explained that her logic was that you put vanilla and eggs together when you make French toast, so why wouldn't it work? She was so funny without trying to be. She continued to describe her cooking skills. She told us sometimes she would make a dish, and it would turn out amazing; other times she wasn't as successful. Her husband fondly referred to her creations as "Katy's Concoctions." Sadly, she lost her dear husband. Through her loss, we have become good friends. I'm so grateful to have overheard her conversation that day in the pool.

Thankfully, I am currently celebrating three years in remission. Two more years and I will be considered cured. During that time, we hope to be traveling this country seeing new places and meeting friends we haven't met yet. We want to be "story collectors." Everyone has a story, and we want to share the stories we come across on our YouTube channel. Please follow along: @theplacesyougowithcarrieandjoe.

It may sound strange, but the worst day of my life has turned into the best day of my life. Finding out that I had leukemia was the scariest thing I have ever gone through. Knowing that only one out of three people have survived what I've been through makes it so surreal. The blessings we have experienced far outweigh the disease. If I hadn't gotten sick, we would have never been able to experience the outpouring of love we received. Family and friends were there for us, but the support from complete strangers has humbled us. To say thank you seems so insignificant compared to the generous acts and kindnesses we received. The bonus is the new perspective we have living our lives. Creating memories is a priority. When I look in the mirror and see gray hair and wrinkles, I no longer cringe. I celebrate that I am still here to see them. They are a sign that I am getting older and that is a good thing! I never would have had the chance to feel the level of love and support I experienced from the person who matters most to me in this world—my husband.

The one drawback to getting better and being in remission is that the phone calls to check on you become less frequent. My kids don't call me as much; nor do my siblings. It's a tradeoff that I am willing to accept. I'll take my good health and fewer phone calls over sickness and constant contact to see how I am doing.

I hope our challenges and experiences have made us kinder, more compassionate people. We try to remember that everyone goes through difficult times, and we never know what someone is going through when we meet them. We are not the same people we used to be, thank goodness! We have grown and evolved into the people we are today and look forward to many more years of making memories together!

We have learned that all struggles have a purpose. It may be to give you more life experience or maybe it's just to make you better or stronger. One thing is for sure, we all have them.

It might sound harsh, but the truth is, we are all dying. Every day we are all one day closer to leaving this world. We all have one less day to spend on this earth. This keeps things in perspective for me. When I don't feel like doing anything, I tell myself that God did not give me one more day to just lie around and do nothing. I live with a sense of urgency to accomplish my goals and dreams. My life includes the need to express love now, not later. It's the knowledge that I am going to eventually die that helps me focus on being alive.

Love conquers all…

Several years ago, I watched a movie on TV. It was called "Into the Wild." It had a profound message. The main character discovers that true happiness can be found only when shared with others. I'd like to think I have shared my happiness with you.

There is an amazing soul that I follow on Instagram. She goes by Nightbirde. She was a contestant on the show *America's Got Talent*. She was battling cancer and had a two percent chance of survival. Most of us would consider that lousy odds. She, on the other hand, said, "Two percent? That's better than zero, right?" She posted a saying that I feel deeply. She said, "You can't wait until life isn't hard any more to be happy." Sadly, just as I was finishing this book, Nightbirde passed away at the age of 31. But during her short life, she was an inspiration to many with her lessons on living life to the fullest.

As I was trying to wrap this book up and get it published, I experienced a scary few days. Following an UTI (urinary tract infection), I could not get my energy back. I spent ten days with fatigue and headaches. Those were the initial symptoms that originally sent me to the ER before I was diagnosed with Leukemia. I had just had my bloodwork done four weeks prior and everything looked fine so I kept on reminding myself of that. But, with each passing day, my mind started playing the "what if" game. What if my Leukemia did come back? What would I do? I am pretty sure I wouldn't go through another bone marrow transplant. When I first saw my doctor at the Mayo Clinic, I told him he had one shot. I know I would be choosing the shorter life, but we would make the best of however much time we had left together. I don't want Joe's last memories to be of me being weak and sick. Watching him care for me, kills me! I want to be his wife, not his patient. While we were waiting for new bloodwork, we were planning our escape should the results show the leukemia had in fact returned. As we drove to the doctor's office for my blood draw, Joe and I both had tears in our eyes fearing the worst. I can't express the relief we felt once we got the results in our hands. Everything still looked fine. My body was just fighting off a virus. I can't express the relief we felt. The scare did put some things into perspective for us though. We have been patiently waiting for me to turn 65 so I could go on Medicare. With my decision not to undergo more treatment, we really don't need to base our retirement on insurance. We are actively purging the last of our belongings and preparing to start our travels.

I'M NOT afraid of dying… I'm afraid of not living![1]

1.

ABOUT THE AUTHOR

After helping Carrie edit this book, she asked me to write the "About the Author" section. I eagerly accepted, knowing that this would not be your typical "About the Author" paragraph. Sure, I can tell you where she was born, how many children she has and that she is embarking on an RV journey around the country with her beloved husband, Joe. But as you will discover or have discovered reading this book, Carrie is so much more than that. Carrie is a hero.

I was one of those people Carrie described who did not hang out with her in high school. I was aware of her in my classes and as head majorette while I was in the marching band, but we were never close. We connected when I reached out to her after seeing a post about her gastric bypass surgery as I was considering the same surgery. We had a long talk on the phone, and she shared the pros and cons with me. After that, we continued to communicate through Facebook, phone calls and even snail mail.

From a distance, I watched her battle with Leukemia and tried to support her as best I could through cards and gifts and—most importantly—love and prayers. I was so struck by her courage and positive attitude as she fought for her life. It has been a joy to work on this book with her. In July, she and I will check off an item on both of our bucket lists—to see a Red Sox game at Fenway Park together. The tickets for a game against the Yankees are already purchased.

I recently read a review of Delia Ephon's new book *Life on Tenth: A Second Chance at Life* in *the New York Times*. I immediately purchased it, and it is at the top of my pile of books to read. Delia has successfully fought the same battle as Carrie. In the review, Ephron is quoted as saying, "You end up in the situation, and you just do what you do." That's Carrie.

Her husband, Peter Rutter, responded, "Actually, Delia, that is the **essence of being heroic**. You persist even if it seems impossible." That's Carrie.

Deb Noack

April 25, 2022